Charles King

Laramie

Or, the Queen of Bedlam

Charles King

Laramie
Or, the Queen of Bedlam

ISBN/EAN: 9783337130411

Printed in Europe, USA, Canada, Australia, Japan

Cover: Foto ©ninafisch / pixelio.de

More available books at **www.hansebooks.com**

OR,

THE QUEEN OF BEDLAM.

A

STORY OF THE SIOUX WAR OF 1876.

BY

CAPTAIN CHARLES KING, U.S.A.,

AUTHOR OF "THE COLONEL'S DAUGHTER," "MARION'S FAITH," "THE DESERTER," "FROM THE RANKS," ETC.

PHILADELPHIA:
J. B. LIPPINCOTT COMPANY.
1889.

Copyright, 1889, by J. B. Lippincott Company.

"LARAMIE."
OR,
THE QUEEN OF BEDLAM.

A STORY OF FRONTIER ARMY LIFE.

I.

THE snow had gone from all the foot-hills and had long since disappeared in the broad river bottom. It was fast going from the neighboring mountains, too—both the streams told plainly of that, for while the Platte rolled along in great, swift surges under the Engineer Bridge, its smaller tributary—the "Larmie," as the soldiers called it—came brawling and foaming down its stony bed and sweeping around the back of the fort with a wild vehemence that made some of the denizens of the south end decidedly nervous. The rear windows of the commanding officer's house looked out upon a rushing torrent, and where the surgeon lived, at the south-west angle, the waters lashed against the shabby old board fence that had been built in by-gone days, partly to keep the children and chickens from tumbling into the stream when the water was high, partly to keep out marauding coyotes when the water was low. South and west the bare, gray-brown slopes shut out the horizon and limited the view. Eastward lay the broad, open valley beyond the confluence of the streams,—bare and level along the crumbling banks, bare and rolling along the line of the foot-hills. Northward the same brown ridges were tumbled up like a mammoth wave a mile or so beyond the river, while between the northern limits of the garrison proper and the banks of the larger stream there lay a level "flat," patched here and there with underbrush, and streaked by a winding tangle of hoof- and wheel-tracks that crossed and re-crossed each other, yet led, one and all, to the distant bridge that spanned the stream, and thence bore away northward like the tines of a pitchfork, the one to the right going over the hills a three days' march to the Indian agencies up along the "Wakpa Schicha," the other leading more to the west around a rugged shoulder of bluff, and then stretching away due north for the head-waters of the Niobrara and the shelter of the jagged flanks of Rawhide Butte. Only in shadowy clusters up and down the stream was there anywhere sign of timber. Foliage, of course, there was none. Cottonwood and willow in favored nooks along the Platte were just beginning to shoot forth their tiny pea-green tendrils in answer to the caressing touch of the May-day sunshine.

April had been a month of storm and bluster and huge, wanton wastes of snow, whirling and drifting down from the bleak range that veiled the valley of the Laramie from the rays of the westering sun; and any one who chose to stroll out from the fort and climb the gentle slope to the bluffs on that side, and to stand by the rude scaffolding whereon were bleaching the bones of some Dakota brave, could easily see the gleaming, glistening sides of the grand old peak, fully forty miles away,—all one sheen of frosty white that still defied the melting rays. Somebody was up there this very afternoon,—two somebodies. Their figures were blacked in silhouette against the sky close by the Indian scaffolding; but even at the distance one could see they were not Indian mourners. That was not a blanket which the tall, slender shape had just thrown about the slighter form. Mrs. Miller, the major's wife, who happened to be crossing the parade at the moment, knew very well that it was an officer's cape, and that Randall McLean had carefully wrapped it about Nellie Bayard lest the keen wind from the west, blowing freely over the ridges, should chill the young girl after her long spin across the prairie and up the heights.

A good-hearted woman was Mrs. Miller, and very much did she like the doctor's sweet and pretty daughter, very much better than she fancied the doctor himself, although, had she been pressed for a reason for her distrust of the senior medical attendant of the garrison, Mrs. Miller might have found it hard to give satisfactory answer. He was a widower, and "that made him interesting to some people," was her analysis of the situation. She really knew nothing more detrimental to his character, and yet she wished he had not lost his wife, and her wishes on this point were not entirely because of Elinor's motherless state. It was the first year the girl had spent in garrison since the death of that loving mother nearly a decade before. There were not lacking hearts full of sympathy and affection for the weeping little maiden when that sore affliction befell her. She had been taken to her mother's old home, reared and educated, and possibly over-indulged there, and sometimes gladdened by visits from her handsome and distinguished father. A marked man in his profession was Dr. Bayard, one of the "swells" of the medical corps of the army, and rapturously had he been loved by the beautiful and delicate woman whose heart he had won, somewhat to the sorrow of her people. They did not like the army, and liked it still less in the long years of separation that followed. Bayard was a man who in his earlier service had secured many a pleasant detail, and had been a society leader at Old Point Comfort, and Newport, and Boston Harbor, and now, in his advancing years and under an administration with which he had lost influence, he was taking his turn at frontier service, and heartily damning the fates that had landed him at Laramie. His dead wife's father was a man whose dictum was law in the political party in power. The doctor appealed to him to urge the Secretary of War to revoke the orders which consigned him to the isolation of a Wyoming post, but the old gentleman had heard more than one account of his widowed son-in-law's propensities and peccadilloes. It was his conviction that Newport was not the place for handsome Dr. Bayard; he rather delighted in the news that the doctor promptly sent him; but, though a power in politics, he was in some things no politician, for, when his son-in-law begged him to use his influence in his behalf, the old gentleman said no,—and told him why.

That gloomy November when Dr. Bayard left for the West he took his revenge on the old people, for he took his daughter with him.

It was a cruel, an almost savage blow, and one that was utterly unlooked for. Fond as he had been of Elinor's mother, and proud as he was of his pretty child, the doctor had been content to spend only occasional holidays with her. Every few months he came to visit them, or had her run down to New

York for a brief tour among the shops, the theatres, and the picture-galleries. She was enthusiastically devoted to him, and thought no man on earth so grand, so handsome, so accomplished. She believed herself the most enviable of daughters as the child of so fond and indulgent a father. She gloried in the pride which he manifested in her success at school, in her budding beauty and graceful ways. She welcomed his coming with infinite delight, and was ever ready to drop any other project when papa's brief letters and telegrams summoned her to the city. Whatever their feeling toward the doctor, her grandparents had never betrayed them to her or sought to undermine—or rather undeceive—her loyal devotion; but never had it occurred to them as a possibility that he would assert his paternal claim and bear away with him the idol of their hearts, the image of the cherished daughter he had won from them so many years before. Proud old judge and senator as he was, the grandfather had never been so sore stricken. He could not plead, could not humble himself to unbend and ask for mercy. For good and sufficient cause he had denied his son-in-law the boon that had been so confidently demanded, and in his chagrin and exasperation Dr. Bayard had taken his revenge. It was too late now to prepare their little Elinor for characteristics of which she had never dreamed, too late to warn her that her superb father was not the hero her fancy painted. In utter consternation, in wretchedness of spirit, the old couple saw her borne away, tearful at leaving them, yet blissful at being with papa, and going once more to the army, and they could only pray heaven to guard her and to comfort them.

But, if Dr. Bayard was incensed at being ordered to so distant a station as Laramie, in the first place, his discontent was greatly augmented with the coming of the new year. It was a crowded post when he and Elinor arrived in the early winter, but long before the snows had begun to disappear all the cavalry, and all but two companies of infantry there on duty, were ordered northward into the Sioux country, and his assistant was taken with the field column, leaving to the older man the unwelcome task of caring for the families of all the absentees as well as for the few men in the hospital. The sight of Dr. Bayard, dignified, handsome, elegant in dress and manner, tramping about in the deep snow around the laundresses' quarters was one that afforded rather too much malicious delight to a few of the denizens of the club-room at the store; but the contemplation of his own misfortunes was beginning to bring the doctor himself to a state of mind still less justifiable. All his life he had shunned the contemplation of poverty and distress. He was now for the first time seeing sickness and suffering in surroundings that had nothing of refinement, and he shrank, like the sensitive and selfish creature that he was, from such contamination.

It was hard news for Laramie when the telegraph flashed the tidings of the savage fight up among the snows in the Powder River country, but it was comfort to Dr. Bayard. He had begged for an assistant to replace the young surgeon who had been taken to the front, and his request was declined on the ground that the size of the present garrison did not warrant the detail of an additional medical officer. Bayard ground his teeth, and swore, when the paper came back to him, "Respectfully transmitted with attention invited to the endorsement of the medical director,—which is approved." He could have testified under oath now, so strong was his conviction, that his father-in-law, the surgeon-general of the army, and the medical director of the department were all in league to annoy and humiliate him to the verge of distraction—or resignation from the service. But the fight with Crazy Horse's band of Sioux brought unexpected aid and comfort to the doctor in greatly adding to his responsibilities; a large number of wounded and frozen soldiers were being brought in as fast as ambulance and *travois* could haul them, and now he was shrewd enough to know that an assistant would have to be sent, and he did not even ask. The young doctor who came back with the wounded was himself so badly frozen when only two days' march away that he could be of no further aid. Bayard went forward through the snow-drifts up the Platte to meet his new patients, saw them safely housed in hospital, and gave himself up to the devoted efforts in their behalf. The moment the assistant arrived he was given instructions to take entire charge of the soldiers' families and the "hangers on" of the post.

And now the 1st of May was come; many of the wounded were well enough to be hobbling around the fort in search of air and sunshine; many additional troops had passed Laramie on their way up to the front and many more were expected, but there still remained only the two infantry companies to "hold the fort." At the earliest intimation of trouble there had come back from the East, where he had been spending the first long leave he had enjoyed in some years of service, a stalwart young lieutenant by the name of McLean. Border warfare had no more charm for him than it had for any other soldier who remembered that it was one in which the Indian had everything to win and nothing to lose. He had seen not a little of it, with hard marching, scouting, and suffering, through winter's cold and summer's heat, in more than one campaign in the recent past. It was hard to give up the leave, but harder to have his regiment take the field without him. It was with a sense of having been defrauded in some measure, therefore, that he found himself retained at the fort, simply because his own company happened to be kept back on guard. The column had gone when he succeeded in reaching the post, and his chagrin was bitter when he found that, so far from following and overtaking them on the trail to the Big Horn, he was ordered to assume command of his company in the place of Captain Bruce, who, though present at the fort, was rapidly breaking down with rheumatic trouble that confined him to his quarters. McLean went to the major commanding, he also wrote to his colonel and telegraphed to the adjutant, but all to no purpose. There must be an officer with each company, even though it be only a post-guard, and it was his ill-luck to have to be the man.

And yet, three weeks after his return, Mr. McLean was by no means the disgusted and unhappy subaltern he declared himself, and it was a fact patent to all the garrison that Nellie Bayard was the source of comfort which reconciled him to the situation.

The fort was crowded with officers' families at the

time. A large force had been maintained here during the winter, and when the troops took the field in March the ladies and children remained,—a sacred charge for Major Miller and his two companies of "foot." Not only was this the case, but such was the threatening and truculent bearing of all the Sioux and Cheyenne Indians remaining at the agency on White River to the north-east, that a few of the officers on duty at Fort Robinson (the post established there to overlook and overawe (?) the savages) had sent their families back to Laramie under escort, and those gentle refugees were received and housed and welcomed with a hospitality and warmth that one never sees outside the army. Every set of officers' quarters, therefore, was crowded to its full capacity, and a thing that never before had happened in the chronicles of the old frontier post was now a matter of course. Even "Bedlam," the ramshackle, two-story frame rookery, once sacred to the bachelor element, had now two families quartered therein, and one of these comprised the wife, maiden sister, and three children of Captain Forrest, of the cavalry,— "refugees from Robinson." For several days after their arrival they had been housed under Major Miller's roof,—all the other quarters, except Dr. Bayard's, being crowded,—and Nellie Bayard had begged her father to invite Mrs., Miss, and the little Forrests to make his house their home. The doctor willingly accorded her permission to invite Miss Forrest, but drew the line at her unattractive sister-in-law and the more than unattractive trio of youngsters. Before she had known Miss Forrest three days, however, Nellie Bayard felt less eagerness to ask her to be her guest, and Mrs. Miller, as kind and generous a soul as ever lived, had gone so far as to say to her, "Don't."

And yet it seemed so unkind, so utterly lacking in hospitality or courtesy. After his second call at the commanding officer's, and a sprightly chat with this beaming, bright-eyed, vivacious young woman, Dr. Bayard had rather pointedly inquired,—

"Nellie, dear, I thought you were to invite Miss Forrest to pay you a visit; have you done so?"

"No, papa," was the hesitating answer. "I did mean to—but—don't you expect Dr. and Mrs. Graham early next week? You know you'll have to ask them."

"Oh, I know that, child, but the house is big. There are two spare rooms, and even if we had to take in more, you two might share your room awhile, might you not?"

"We might, papa dear; but—I'm afraid I don't like her. That is, she doesn't attract me as she did at first. I thought her charming then."

"Tut, tut, tut! Why, what on earth's the matter with my little woman?" asked the doctor, bending down over her as they were walking home. "It isn't like you, Nell, to be censorious. What's she been doing?—making eyes at young McLean?"

He might have judged better than that, had he reflected an instant. He never yet had thought of his daughter except as a mere child, and he did not mean for an instant to intimate that her growing interest in the young lieutenant was anything more than a "school-girl" fancy. She was old enough, however, to take his thoughtless speech *au sérieux*, and it hurt her.

"Papa!" was her one, indignant word of remonstrance. She would not even defend herself against such accusation.

"I know!—I understand—I didn't mean it except as the merest joke, my child," he hurriedly interposed. "I thought you'd laugh at the idea."

But she would not speak of it, and he quickly sought to change the subject, never even asking other reason for her apparent aversion to Miss Forrest. It was true that the speedy coming of Dr. and Mrs. Graham would make it necessary that he should open his doors to an officer of his own corps and profession.

For a few days, however, that thoughtless speech seemed to rankle in his gentle daughter's soul.

Never before had she known hesitancy or embarrassment in her daily, hourly chat with that fondly loved father. Now there was a topic that she could not approach. Hitherto she used to tell him all about her walks and talks with Mr. McLean. That young gentleman, indeed, had accompanied them the evening they went to the major's to call upon the latest arrival among the refugees, but now she shrank from mentioning either Miss Forrest or him. For several days after that talk it seemed as though she avoided not only the subjects, but the two persons themselves. At least both of them would have sworn to the latter part of the statement, and McLean was at his wit's end to account for it.

Meantime, there being nowhere else to go, the Forrests had moved into "Bedlam" in the same hallway with the family of Lieutenant Post, also refugees from Robinson; but while the Posts occupied rooms on the lower floor, the Forrests took the four chambers overhead. Two young cavalry officers were the occupants up to the outbreak of the campaign, but all their furniture and "traps" were summarily moved over to the quartermaster's storehouse by order of the commanding officer,—and one trip of one wagon did the entire job,—for the emergency was one that called for action, and Major Miller was a man to meet it. The Forrests and the Posts, therefore, were now sole occupants of the south end of "Bedlam," and Lieutenant McLean's two rooms were on the ground-floor of the north end. The hall-ways ran entirely through from east to west, giving on the west side into court-yards separated from each other by a high board fence and completely enclosed by one of similar make. On the east side, fronting the roadway, were broad verandas on both first and second floors, and these were common property of the occupants of both halls. By the rear or west door they could not pass from one hall to the other, on account of the intervening fence. By the east door the veranda on either story formed a convenient thoroughfare. McLean occupied the two rooms on the north side of this hall, and a brother infantryman, also a bachelor, occupied the two above him. The opposite rooms on both floors were the garrison homes of married officers now in the fields with their commands, and their doors were kept locked by the quartermaster. The Forrests and Posts, with the Bedouin-like ease of long experience on the frontier, had established a dining-room in common on the ground-floor of the south end, and the temporary kitchen was knocked up in the back yard. The south division, therefore, contained a lively colony of women and children; the north halls, only empty rooms and two lone bachelors.

This very May-day afternoon on which our story opens, as Lieutenant McLean and Miss Bayard started forth on their stroll, Miss Forrest, with a shawl hugged woman-fashion around her shapely form, was taking a constitutional up and down the upper gallery. She came to the railing and bent down, beaming, smiling, and kissing her hand to them,—and a winsome smile she had,—then, as they passed out along the walk by the old ordnance storehouse, she stood for a time looking after them.

That night, just after dusk, when Mr. McLean came bounding up the front steps, intent on getting an album from his quarters, and then returning to Mrs. Miller's, where he was spending the evening, he was surprised to find the lamp extinguished. All was darkness as he opened the front door. So, too, on the second floor there was no light in the hall, and yet he could have sworn that both lamps were burning when he went out at eight o'clock, half an hour before. In his own room, the front one, however, the very opposite was the case. He had turned the lamp low the last thing before starting, and closed the front of his standing desk, turning the key in the lock. He always did these things when leaving his quarters at night. Now the hanging lamp was throwing a steady light all over the simple, soldier room, and the desk was wide open.

The rear room, his bedchamber, was dark as usual, and his first thought was for his papers. These were in their pigeon-holes, undisturbed. Two drawers had been pulled open; one was now half closed, while the other remained with almost its full length, lying, tipped out, upon the shelving desk. It was filled with Lynchburg tobacco, a bright-colored, fragrant brand much affected by pipe-smokers at that time, and an idea occurred to him. He stepped out into the hall and shouted up the stairs,—

"Hat!—O-o-o, Hatton! You been here?"

No answer.

Mr. McLean shook his head in perplexity. He and his comrade, Lieutenant Hatton, were intimates who smoked many a pipe together out of that same drawer. He had many a time bidden the latter to come in and help himself whenever he wanted to. Bachelor doors are always open in the army, and the desk key was generally in the lock. Still it was not like Hatton to leave things in disorder behind him, even if he were to take McLean at his word. No! It wasn't Hatton, unless something very unforeseen had suddenly called him away. Stepping quickly back into the room he felt a draught of cool air, and saw that the portière that hung between the two rooms was bulging slightly toward him. Instantly he stepped into his bedroom, where all was dark, struck a match, and saw, the moment its flash illumined surrounding objects, that the one door he generally kept locked was now ajar. It led into the hall, and thither strode McLean. Up to this instant not a sound had he heard. Now, fairly flying up the old, creaky stairs, light as kittens', quick as terriers', yet stealthy, almost noiseless, he distinctly heard slippered footfalls. They whirled at the head of the stairs, and flashed through the hall-way overhead and out on the front veranda, and he, instead of pursuing, stood stone still, rooted to the floor, his heart beating hard, his hands clinching in amaze. What stunned him was the fact that with the footfalls went the swish of dainty silken skirts.

II.

It was full ten minutes before Mr. McLean reissued from his quarters on his return to the major's house. In the mean time he had searched his desk and summed up his losses. They amounted to mere trifles—a few postage-stamps and perhaps five dollars in currency—which happened to be lying in the drawer above his tobacco receptacle. "Lucky I hadn't got my April pay yet!" thought he. There were some handsome sleeve-buttons and a scarf-pin or two in another drawer, but these had not been touched,—the pilferer had been interrupted too soon. Some letters and notes that were lying in the lower pigeon-holes had evidently been objects of scrutiny, but were still there—so far as he had time to count. He had left a jolly little gathering at the Millers', and he was eager to return; he had left them only at Mrs. Miller's urgent request that he should bring over his "scrap-book," in which he had a miscellaneous assortment of photographs of army friends and army scenes, of autographs, doggerel rhymes, and newspaper clippings, such as "Spelling Tests" and "Feats in Pronunciation," and a quantity of others containing varied and useful information. It was a great stand-by and resource of his, and had helped to while away many an evening on the frontier. Now, Mrs. Miller had been telling Nellie Bayard about it, and was eager that she should see it. The major, too, and several ladies present, all united in the request and enjoined upon him to hurry back. As "Bedlam" lay but a hundred yards away, there was no reason why he should not have returned in five minutes, but it was fifteen when he reappeared, and was, as became the only young man in the room, the immediate centre of combined question and invective.

"What could have kept you so long?" "Where on earth have you been?" "Were it anybody but Mr. McLean, I would say he had gone down to the club-room for a drink," etc. Nellie Bayard alone was silent. The question that occurred to her was finally asked by Mrs. Miller,—

"Why, Mr. McLean, how white you look! Have you seen a ghost?"

"No," he answered, laughing nervously. "I've seen nothing. It is dark as Erebus outside, and I ran into something I couldn't see at all,—something too tangible for a ghost."

"Who was it or what was it?"

"That's what I'm dying to know. I was out in the very middle of the parade, and this something was scurrying over toward Gordon's quarters as I was coming here. We ran slap into each other. I sang out, 'Halloo! Beg pardon,' and began hunting for the book that was knocked out from under my arm, and this figure just whizzed right on,—never answered at all."

"Odd!" said the major. "Some one of the men, do you think? been over paying a visit to a sweetheart in some kitchen of the opposite quarters?"

"Well, no," answered McLean, coloring and hesitating. "It might have been some sweetheart going over to visit the east side and taking a short cut across the parade. It wasn't a man."

"Oh! That's it, of course," chimed in Mrs. Brenham at once. "The Johnsons have a girl—Winnie they call her—who is perpetually gadding about, and I warrant it was she. Come! Let us see the scrap-book."

And so the party returned to the business of the evening and were soon absorbed in the pages of McLean's collection. He had many a question to answer, and was kept from the seat he longed to take, by Nellie Bayard's side. Where three or four women are gathered together over an album of photographs or a scrap-book of which he is the owner, no man need hope to escape for so much as an instant. Yet she was watching him and wondering at what she saw,—the effort it cost him to pay attention to their simplest question—the evident distraction that had seized upon him.

By and by tattoo sounded. The major went out with McLean to receive the reports, and when they returned Mr. Hatton came too.

"Where have you been, Mr. Hatton?" asked Mrs. Miller. "We've been looking for you all the evening, and wouldn't have a bite or a glass of wine until you came in."

"Over at the Gordons'. They are having a little gathering too, mostly of the refugees,—regular hen convention. I was the only man there for over an hour."

"Who all were there?" inquired the hostess—her Southern birth and her woman's interest in the goings-on of the garrison manifesting themselves at one and the same time.

"Oh, about a dozen, all told," answered Mr. Hatton. "Mrs. Bruce and Jeannie, Mrs. Forrest, Mrs. Post, the Gordon girls, Mrs. Wells, and finally Miss Forrest. The little parlor was packed like a ration-can by nine o'clock, and I was glad to slip away at first call."

"A likely statement in view of the fact that Jeannie Bruce was there."

"Fact, though!" answered Hatton, with a knowing look on his handsome face. He did not want to say it was because Jeannie Bruce went home at "first call" and that he escorted her.

McLean would be sure to understand that point, however, thought Mr. Hatton to himself, and to obviate the possibility of his mischievously suggesting that solution of the matter it might be well to tip him a wink. Looking around in search of his chum, Mr. Hatton was surprised at the odd and wretched expression on McLean's face. The tall young subaltern had seated himself at last by Nellie Bayard's side, but instead of devoting himself to her, as was to have been expected, he was staring with white face at Hatton and drinking in every word.

"Why, what's the matter, old man? You look all struck of a heap!" exclaimed Hatton, in genuine concern.

"Mr. McLean encountered a spook on his way over here," laughed the major, seeing that McLean, in embarrassment, knew not how to reply. "He ran afoul of a flying Dutchwoman out on the parade in the dark, and was mystified because she would not stop and chat with him."

"What nonsense, major!" sharply interposed his better half. "You know we settled it long ago that that must have been the Johnsons' Winnie on one of her gad-abouts. Why do you add to the mischief?"

"Hm!" responded her lord in a broad grin. "Coming from a woman, that is a stinger. Can't a fellow have a little fun at McLean's expense without being accused of scattering scandal?"

"You are only too ready to accuse one of us of starting malicious stories," replied his wife, with honest indignation. "It might be as well for you to consider the possible effect of your own words."

"What possible effect—ill effect, that is—could my remark have had even if repeated?" demanded the major in amusement.

"Well, never you mind now; I'm glad we all understand one another here at any rate," answered Mrs. Miller, earnestly. "Now let us have peace and a truce to the spook story. Mrs. Taylor, now won't you sing?"

"Really, Mrs. Miller, I ought not to stay another moment. I left the nurse in charge of my babies, and I know perfectly well that by this time she is out at the back gate flirting with Sergeant Murray. Indeed, Mr. McLean, I do wish you would confine that altogether-too-utterly-attractive young man to the limits of the barracks. He's at our gate morn, noon, and night, and whenever he's there my Maggie is there too, and the children might scream themselves hoarse and she never hear. Why, I'm a perfect slave! I can't go anywhere. It's just do for those precious babies from dawn till midnight. I might as well have no nurse at all. Oh, no, indeed, Mrs. Miller. I must go this minute. Indeed I must. But, Mr. Hatton, how did it happen that Miss Forrest only came in late?"

"More than I know, Mrs. Taylor. She said she was unable to come earlier on account of letters or something. I didn't pay much attention. You see there were six women around me already. I've never known the bliss of being an undoubted belle until this spring."

"Then I suppose, too, she stopped to dress. You know Fanny Forrest has such beautiful dresses, Mrs. Miller, and she's hardly had a chance to show one of them since she got here. What did she wear this evening, Mr. Hatton?"

"'Pon my soul, I don't know. It was a dress, of course, blue or green—or something."

"Yes—something, undoubtedly; but what was it like? Did it——?"

"The idea of asking me to describe a woman's dress! Why, I don't know a poplin from a polonaise, though I suppose there's a distinction of some kind. All I know is that this one shimmered and had things all over it like No. 12 shot or Sioux moccasin beads, and it swished and rustled as she walked through the hall and up the stairs."

"Oh, I know,—that long silk princesse—electric blue—that came from New York last October and —— Beg pardon. What?"

"Not you, Mrs. Taylor. Go on!" said Mrs. Miller, pleasantly. "Mr. Hatton's servant has just called for him at the door. Wants to see him a moment." And Hatton left the parlor with the major at his heels.

An hour later, after seeing Nellie Bayard home, and striving in vain to be like his actual self, Mr. McLean hurried to his quarters. Just as he expected, Hatton was standing in front of the open fireplace puffing furiously at a chunky little brierwood pipe. He looked up from under his heavy eyebrows as McLean came in, but said nothing. The occupant of the room filled and lighted his own particular "cutty," and threw himself into an easy chair, first divesting himself of the handsome uniform "blouse" he had worn during the evening, and getting into an easy old shooting-jacket. Then through a cloud of fragrant smoke the two men looked silently at each other. It was Hatton who spoke first:

"Well, Mac."

"What's up, Hatton?"

"Missed anything to-night?"

"Nothing to speak of," answered McLean, coloring. He had the hatred of his race for the faintest equivocation.

"Well, I have, and I thought you might have been visited likewise. My bureau and dressing-case have been ransacked and I'm out a good two hundred dollars' worth.

"The devil you say!"

"Have you lost nothing?"

"Five dollars or so,—as I said, nothing I wanted to mention."

"Why?"

"Well—because."

"A woman's reason, Mac."

"How do you know a woman's the reason?" asked McLean, almost fiercely, as he started from the chair. He had only imperfectly heard his friend's muttered words.

"I don't!—and that isn't what I said," replied Hatton, coolly. "But see here,—now we've got down to it," and he stopped to emit two or three voluminous puffs of smoke from under his thick moustache. "It would appear that the thief went through the next-door premises despite the presence of nurses and servants and children,—and then dropped some of his plunder here. Eh?" and he held forth a dainty handkerchief.

McLean took it, his hands trembling, and a creeping, chilling sensation running through his fingers. It was of finest fabric, sheer and soft and very simply embroidered. It was without, rather than with, surprise he found the letters "F. F." in one corner. He raised it, and, not knowing what to say for the moment, sat there inhaling the delicate fragrance that hung about the white folds.

"Where'd you find it?" he finally asked.

"Just at the foot of your bureau, Mac. It was lying there when I came in, half an hour ago."

"Then it's mine to dispose of at least," said McLean, as he rose promptly from his chair, stepped quickly to the fireplace, and tossed the dainty toy among the flames. The next instant the last vestige of it was swept from sight, and the two men stood looking quietly into each other's eyes.

III.

The compact little post of Fort Laramie looked hardly big enough to contain its population two days afterward when, under the influence of a warm sunshine and the sweet music of the band, all the women and children seemed to have gathered around the parade. Guard-mounting was just over, and the adjutant had ordered the musicians to stop and play a few airs in honor of its being the first morning on which it was warm enough for the men to appear without overcoats and the women without their furs. The little quadrangle, surrounded as it was by quarters and houses of every conceivable pattern except that which was modern and ornamental, was all alive with romping children and with sauntering groups of ladies chatting with the few cavaliers who happened to be available. A small battalion of infantry had marched up from the nearest railway-station at Cheyenne, a good hundred miles away, and pitched its tents on the flat to the north of the post, and this brought a few visiting officers into the enclosure; otherwise, except old Bruce, there would have been no man to talk to, as Hatton and McLean were "marching on" and "marching off" guard respectively, and the surgeon, adjutant, and quartermaster were all engaged in the old head-quarters office with Major Miller.

While many of the ladies were seated in the sunshine on the piazzas, and even "Bedlam" was so ornamented, there were several who were strolling up and down the board and gravel walks, and of these Fanny Forrest was certainly the most striking in appearance. She was tall, stately in carriage, and beautifully formed. Her head was carried proudly and her features were regular and fine. "But for that hardness of expression she might be a tearing beauty," was the comment of more than one woman who knew and envied her; but that expression certainly existed and to her constant detriment. All manner of conjectures had been started to account for her somewhat defiant air and that hard, set look that so rarely left her face except when she smiled and strove to please. No one really knew much about her. Captain Forrest, her brother, was one of the popular men of his regiment, who years before had become enamoured of and *would* marry the namby-pamby though pretty daughter of the old post chaplain. She happened to be the only young lady in the big garrison of McPherson, one of those long winters just after the War of the Rebellion, and Forrest was susceptible. Her prettiness had soon faded, and there was no other attraction to eke it out; but her husband was big-hearted and gentle, and he strove hard not to let her see he thought her changed. Still, she was a querulous, peevish woman by this time, poor girl, and her numerous olive-branches had been more than a stronger woman could have managed. Forrest's house was not the jolliest in the garrison, and he was given to drifting away as a consequence; but the previous summer there came to him news that took him suddenly Eastward. He was gone a month, and when he returned he brought his tall, handsome, stylish sister with him, and it was given out that she was to make her home with him henceforth,—unless, as said the gossips, some other man claimed her. Some other man did,—two some others, in fact, and "a very pretty quarrel as it stood" was only nipped in the bud by the prompt action of the commanding officer at Fort Robinson that very winter. Two young officers had speedily fallen in love with her, and in so doing had fallen out with each other. It was almost a fight, and would have been but for the colonel commanding; and yet it was all absurd, for she turned both of them adrift. Of her past she would not speak, and no one cared to question Forrest. She had been living at her uncle's in New York, was all that any one knew, and finally that had to be changed. She had come out with her bronzed and soldierly brother, and was his guest now; it was evident that there was deep affection between them; it was theorized by the ladies at Robinson that she had had some unlucky love-affair, and this was the more believed after she threw over the two devotees aforementioned. All manner of that alluring bait which women so well know how to use when inviting confidence was thrown to her from time to time, but she refused it and intimacies of any kind, and only one thing saved her from being ostracized by the garrison sisterhood,— her dresses. "She must have had abundant means at some time," said the ladies, "for her dresses are just lovely, and all her clothes are just the same way, very stylish in make and most expensive in material." No woman could quite break friendship with one who had such a mine of fabulous interest in her three Saratogas. Nevertheless, all the letters from Robinson to Laramie, in speaking of her, said she was "worth seeing, but— not attractive." "If anything," wrote one woman, "she is actually repellant in manner to half the ladies in the garrison." This was her status until late that spring, and then came another story,—a queer one, but only Mrs. Bruce received it, and she showed the letter to her husband, who bade her to burn it and say no word of its contents. Ere long another came, —to Mrs. Miller this time,—and spoke of the odd losses sustained by young officers in the garrison. Mr. French, who lived under the same roof with the Forrests, had been robbed twice. No clue to the perpetrator. Then came the spring outbreak of the Sioux, the rush to join Sitting Bull and Crazy Horse, the news of the sharp fight late in March, and the situation at Robinson became alarming. April brought the refugees to Laramie, and here, among others, were the Forrests and the Posts.

And now Miss Forrest was strolling placidly up and down the walk and entirely monopolizing the attention of a tall, fine-looking soldier who had met her for the first time only the previous evening and was evidently eager to resume his place at her side. It was hardly fair to the other women, and they were not slow to remark upon the fact.

"One thing is certain," said Mrs. Gordon, " if I were Nellie Bayard I would not want to have her for a step-mother, and the doctor has been simply devoted to her for the last three days."

"Yes, he seems decidedly smitten, Mrs. Gordon; but did we not hear that Dr. Bayard was always doing the devoted to some woman,—a young one preferred?" asked her next-door neighbor, who had just dropped in for a moment's chat.

"Mrs. Miller certainly told me so; it was his reputation in the East, and very possibly he is attracted now by such an undeniably stylish and handsome girl. She can't be so very young, either. Look at those lines under her eyes."

"Yes, and when she turns her head her neck shows it; the throat is getting stringy. Here comes the doctor from the office now. I warrant he passes every other woman and goes straight to her."

"Then it will be 'good-by, Mr. Mayhew,' to her present escort, I warrant you in return. Fanny Forrest has no use for subalterns except as fun to pass away the time."

"Yet she made eyes at Mr. McLean all that first day she was at the Millers'. I think that is really the reason Mrs. Miller cannot bear her. She won't speak of her if she can help it. Now watch the doctor."

There were perhaps half a dozen ladies in the party at the moment, and all eyes were fastened on the tall and distinguished form of Dr. Bayard as he strode across the parade, his handsome, portly figure showing to excellent advantage in his snug-fitting uniform. They saw him bare his head and bow with courtier-like grace to Miss Forrest and again to her escort as he stopped and extended his hand. Then, after a few words, he again bowed as gracefully as before and passed on in the direction of the hospital.

"Certainly the most elegant man in manner and bearing we have seen at Laramie for I don't know when," said Mrs. Gordon. "I don't wonder Nellie worships him."

"She thinks her father simply perfect," was Mrs.

Wells's reply. "I dread to think what it will cost her when disillusion comes, as come it must. Why! Who is that he is talking with now?"

At the north-west corner of the quadrangle, just beyond "Bedlam," the doctor had encountered a stoutly-built man who wore an overcoat of handsome beaver fur thrown wide open over the chest in deference to the spring-like mildness of the morning, and who carried a travelling-bag of leather in one hand. After a moment of apparently cordial chat the two men walked rapidly southward along the gravel path, all eyes from all the piazzas upon them as they came, and, passing one or two groups of ladies, entered the gateway at the doctor's quarters, where Nellie Bayard with "the Gordon girls" happened to be seated on the veranda. Mrs. Gordon and Mrs. Wells arose from their chairs and gazed across the parade, in their very natural curiosity to see what was going on "over at the doctor's." They saw the stranger raise his cap, and bow low over the hand that Nellie extended to him, and then make a bobbing obeisance to each of the Gordon girls as he was presented to them. Then he took a chair by Miss Bayard's side, while the servant came out and relieved him of his overcoat and bag, and the Gordon girls were seen saying adieu. Nellie followed them to the gate, but they evidently felt that the stranger had not come to see them, and that it was time to leave. The ladies on the home piazza awaited their coming with no little impatience, and Mrs. Gordon was prepared to administer a sharp maternal reproof when they were seen to stop in answer to hails from the groups they passed *en route*. Everybody wanted to know who the fur-coated stranger was, and their progress homeward from the south-west angle was, therefore, nothing short of "running the gauntlet" of interrogations. Possibly in anticipation of the displeasure awaiting her, the elder maiden of the two strove to "cut across lots" when she came near the south-eastern corner, whereat, facing north, stood the big house of the commanding officer; but Mrs. Miller was too experienced a hand, and bore down upon the pair in sudden swoop from her piazza to the front gate, and they had to stop and surrender their information.

As a consequence, every woman along that side of Laramie knew before Mesdames Gordon and Wells that Roswell Holmes, of Chicago, the "wealthy mine-owner and cattle-grower," had just arrived in his own conveyance from Cheyenne, and had been invited to put up at the doctor's quarters during his stay at the fort.

"Think of it!" exclaimed Mrs. Gordon, "a bachelor, only thirty-eight, and worth a million. No wonder Dr. Bayard seized him!"

"The doctor knew him before, mother," put in her

daughter. "Nellie wasn't introduced at all. He came right up and told her how glad he was to see her again,—he looked it, too."

"They knew him in Chicago,—met him there on the way out," said the younger. "I heard the doctor say so. Now, look! Here come Fanny Forrest and Mr. Mayhew, and she wants to know who the stranger is; if she doesn't she's the first person I've met who didn't ask."

But Miss Forrest proved an exception to the rule, so far as questions were concerned, at least. She stopped in front of the gate, looking beamingly up at the group on the piazza.

"Mrs. Gordon," she said, "Mr. Mayhew has invited me to walk down to the camp of the battalion, and, as I haven't been outside the limits of the post since we came, I should like to go. They are to have inspection in 'field kits' in half an hour. Don't you want to come with the girls? He says there are half a dozen young gentlemen down there who are eager to see them———"

"Oh, mamma, do!" implored both girls in a breath.

"Why, I hardly know, Miss Forrest," answered Mrs. Gordon, hesitatingly. "Cannot Mrs. Forrest go?"

"Ruth is never ready to go anywhere," answered Miss Forrest, half laughingly, yet with a certain rueful emphasis. "She is a slave to her babies, and as for Celestine, the nurse, she is no help to her whatever."

"Of course you girls must have a 'matron,'" said Mrs. Gordon. "How long will you be there, Mr. Mayhew?"

"Oh, just about half an hour or so, Mrs. Gordon. Then inspection will be over, and we fellows can all come back with you. It's just for the walk, you know, and the pleasure it will give a raft of second lieutenants." (Mr. Mayhew was a first lieutenant of one year's standing.) "They'll bless me for bringing them down."

"Do let the girls go with us, Mrs. Gordon, and if you are too busy I'll see Ruth at once. I can make Celestine stay home and look after the children, though she cannot; and here come Mr. Hatton and Mr. McLean. One of them, at least, will be glad to join us," said Miss Forrest, with the confidence of handsome womanhood. "Perhaps both of them. No. They are turning off across the parade. Call them, Mr. Mayhew. Let no guilty man escape."

Obediently Lieutenant Mayhew shouted to the two young officers who had just come forth from the presence of the major commanding. Both were in undress uniform and sword-belts; both had caught sight of the tall girl at the Gordons' gate at the same instant, and, had any one disposed to be critical been looking on, that somebody would have been justified in saying they "sheered off" the very next instant so as not to pass her by within speaking distance. Mrs. Miller, sitting where she could see the whole affair, was struck by the sudden change in their line of direction, and watched them in no little curiosity as they halted in recognition of Mayhew's call.

"What is it, Mayhew?" sung out Hatton.

"Come over here a minute, you and McLean. I have a scheme to unfold."

"Can't; I'm officer of the day."

"Well, you come, McLean. Miss Forrest wants to speak with you."

"Mac, there's no way out of it," growled Hatton between his set teeth; "you've got to go."

"Be at the house in ten minutes, then. I'll join you there," said McLean, glancing over his shoulders at his comrade as he started across the springy turf to obey the summons. "What is it, Miss Forrest?" he inquired. "Good-morning Mrs. Gordon—Mrs. Wells—everybody," he continued, as, with forage-cap in hand, he made his obeisance to the various ladies of the party.

"I want you to prove how we Bedlamites stand by one another by placing yourself under my orders for a whole hour. You have no duty or engagement. have you?"

McLean would have given—he knew not what—to be able to say he had; but this *rencontre* was something utterly unlooked for. He could easily have pleaded letters, or company duty, but evasion was a trick he could not brook. "I have none," he quietly answered.

"Then, for the honor of Bedlam, offer your services to these young ladies and be their escort down to camp, where they are dying to go."

"Why, Fanny Forrest! how dare you?" gasped Kate Gordon, the elder.

"Indeed, Miss Forrest, I will not have a detailed escort," indignantly protested Jeannie, the younger.

"What illimitable effrontery!" was the muttered comment of Mrs. Wells, while poor Mrs. Gordon hardly knew what to say or do in her amaze and annoyance. McLean himself had flushed crimson under the combined influence of embarrassment and the recollection of the long talk he and Hatton had had but two nights before. Mayhew, too, could hardly control his surprise, but he declared afterward, when the matter came up for comment down at camp, that he would "give a heap to have that man McLean's self-possession," for with hardly an instant's delay the latter's voice was heard above the voluble protests of the two young ladies,—cordial, kindly, even entreating.

"I should like it, of all things. I want to run down and see the First in the new field rig. Do let the girls go with me, Mrs. Gordon. Come, Miss Kate; come, Miss Jeannie. I'll leave my sword at my quarters as we go."

"Didn't I tell you, Mr. Mayhew?" said Miss Forrest, with heightened color and a confident smile as she took his arm. "It is something to be a queen, if it's only the queen of Bedlam."

And though, rather than create a scene, Mrs. Gordon and her daughters joined the party, and Mrs. Wells and Miss Bruce decided to go, it was noticed then and referred to afterward that Mr. McLean never so much as looked at Miss Forrest or noticed her in any way at the time of this occurrence. It was hardly night before the story had gone all over the garrison, and added to Miss Forrest's growing unpopularity; and it was kind-hearted Mrs. Miller herself who exclaimed, on hearing the details in the inevitably exaggerated form in which all such narrative must travel, "I declare! the title she has assumed seems to fit her,—Queen of Bedlam, indeed!"

IV.

THE doctor was giving a little dinner in honor of his friend Mr. Holmes. Two days now had that gentleman been in garrison, where his advent had created more of a flutter than the coming of an inspector-general. He had a large cattle-range farther to the south, beyond the Chugwater and comparatively removed from the scene of Indian hostility and depredation; but such had become the laxity of discipline on the part of the bureau officials, or such was their dread of their turbulent charges at the reservations, that, from time to time, marauding parties of young warriors had been raiding from the agencies during the month of April, crossing the Platte River and dashing down on the outskirts of the great cattle-herds south of Scott's Bluffs and in the valleys of Horsehead and Bear Creeks. One party had even dared to attack the ranches far up the Chugwater Valley at the crossing of the Cheyenne road; another had ridden all around Fort Laramie, fording the Platte above and below; and several of them had made away with dozens of head of cattle bearing the well-known brand of Mr. Holmes of Chicago. It was to see what could be done toward preventing the recurrence of this sort of thing that brought Mr. Holmes to Laramie. At least he said so, but there were ladies in the garrison who were quick to determine that something worth more to him than a few hundred head of cattle had prompted him to take that dangerous ride up from the railway. "He would never have thought it worth while," said Mrs. Wells after a day of quiet observation, "had Nellie Bayard not been here."

Another thing to give color to this theory was the fact that, yielding to the importunities of Major Miller and his frequent telegraphic reports of Indian dashes on the neighboring ranches, the division commander had ordered a troop of cavalry back from patrol duty around the reservation, and "The Grays" had marched in the very night before. A scouting party of an officer and twenty troopers rode forth that morning with orders to look over the Chugwater and the intervening country around Eagle's Nest. If Mr. Holmes were in a hurry to get back to business, here was excellent opportunity of driving half the way to Cheyenne under escort. But Mr. Holmes, who had been somewhat emphatic in his announcement that he could only stay one day, was apparently well content with his comfortable quarters under the doctor's roof. He might now stay longer, he said, for while up in that part of the country he might just as well look over some mines in the Black Hills, provided there were a chance of getting thither alive. Except for heavily guarded trains, all communication was at an end between the scattered settlements of the Hills and the posts along the Platte and the Union Pacific Railway. The Indians swarmed out from the reservations, attacking everything that appeared along the road, and sometimes capturing the entire "outfit;" after plundering and scalping their victims they built lively fires of the wagons, and cheerfully roasted alive such of their prisoners as had the ill-luck not to be killed in the first place. The road to the Black Hills, either from Sidney or by way of Fort Laramie, was lined with the ashes of burned wagons, and, in lieu of mile-posts, was staked with little, rude, unpainted crosses, each marking the grave of some victim of this savage warfare; and Mr. Holmes was quite right in his theory that it would be far safer and pleasanter to stay at Laramie until some big party went up to the Hills. The doctor was most hospitable in his pressing invitation for him to make his house a home just as long as it might please him. Nellie was glad to win her beloved father's praise by doing what she could to make the army homestead attractive to his guest; the guest himself was courteous, well-bred, and cordial in manner, readily winning friends all over the garrison; and the only man to whom his protracted visit became a matter of serious disquietude was poor Randall Mc-

Lean. With a lover's intuition he saw that the wealthy Chicagoan was deeply interested in sweet Nellie Bayard, and that her father eagerly favored the suit.

Up to the hour of Mr. Holmes's arrival, there was not a day on which the young fellow had not enjoyed a walk or one or more delightful chats with the doctor's pretty daughter. He had no rivals; there were at the moment no other bachelor officers at the post, with the exception of Hatton, who, besides having a chivalrous disposition not to cut in where his comrade was interested, was popularly supposed to be the peculiar property of Miss Janet Bruce.

Now, however, since Mr. Holmes had taken up his abode under the Æsculapian vine and fig-tree, McLean found it simply impossible to see the lady of his love except in general company. The Chicago capitalist, despite his thirty-eight years, was rarely out of reach of the little pink ear, and, though courteous and unobtrusive, it was patent to McLean that he meant no other man should charm it with a lover's wooing until his own substantial claims had had full consideration. No matter at what hour the lieutenant called, there was Roswell Holmes in the parlor; and, when he sought to engage her for a walk, it so happened that papa and Mr. Holmes had arranged to go calling at that very time, and papa had expressed his wish that she should go too. It began to look very ominous before the end of that second day, and when the evening of the dinner came Mr. McLean was decidedly low in his mind. He was not even invited.

Now there was nothing in this circumstance to which he should have attached any importance whatever. Army quarters are small at best, and a dining-room on the frontier big enough to accommodate a dozen people was in those days a decided rarity. The doctor, after consultation with Nellie and with the presiding goddess in the kitchen, had decided upon ten as the proper number to be seated at his table. There would then be no crowding, and all might go off without confusion. Very proud was the doctor of some precious old family plate and some more modern and even more beautiful china with which he adorned his table on state occasions. He wanted to make an impression on his wealthy guest, and this was an opportunity not to be neglected. He gave much thought, too, to the composition of his party. The commanding officer and his wife must, of course, be invited. Captain and Mrs. Bruce he decided upon because they were people of much travel and, for army folks, remarkably well read and informed. They would reflect credit on his entertainment. The adjutant and his wife were also bidden as being guests who would grace his board. But he did not invite even his own junior and assistant, Dr. Weeks. "I can explain all that, Nellie. He won't mind," he said, "and besides, if Holmes can stay till the end of the week, I'll give another and have all the youngsters." She had brightened up at that, for her heart misgave her a little at the thought of her most loyal friends being left out in the cold. Then she looked very grave again when his next words were spoken. "And now, dear, we want one more lady to make our party complete, and no one will do as well as Miss Forrest."

Poor Nellie! She knew not what to say. Her father was, of course, cognizant of the growing dislike to that strange girl, and had pooh-poohed some of the stories that had been brought to his ears. There was not a woman in the officers' quarters whom she would not rather have invited, yet from the very first she felt in the depths of her soul that Miss Forrest would be her father's choice. One timid little suggestion she made in favor of Janet Bruce, since her parents were to be of the party; but the doctor promptly scouted it.

"Why, daughter, she's barely seventeen, a girl who would not be in society at all anywhere in civilization;" and with a sigh Nellie abandoned the point. "Besides," said the doctor as a clincher, "I want this a 'swell' affair; just think how much Miss Forrest's taste in dress will help out."

Certainly his judgment was warranted by her appearance the evening of the dinner, when, the last guest to arrive, Fanny Forrest came rustling down the stairs and into the brightly lighted parlor. It had begun to rain just before sunset, and she had brought Celestine with her to hold the umbrella over her while her own jewelled hands gathered those costly skirts about her under the folds of the gossamer that enveloped her from head to feet. The girl, a bright, intelligent mulattress, followed her mistress up-stairs to the room set apart for the use of the ladies, and was busy removing her wraps when Nellie ran up to inquire if she could be of any assistance.

"Thank you heartily, Nellie," was the cordial answer. "How simply exquisite you look to-night!" and Miss Forrest's winsome smile was brighter than ever as she bent her head to kiss the reluctant cheek that seemed to pale under her touch. "No, run back to your guests. Celestine will put me to rights in a minute, and I'll be down in a jiffy; don't wait."

And so Nellie returned to the parlor, and in a moment Celestine came down and passed out at the front door, and then Miss Forrest's light footfalls could be heard aloft as the guests grouped themselves about the parlor,—the men in their full-dress uniforms, except, of course, their civilian friend,—the ladies in their most becoming dinner toilet. Despite her growing unpopularity every eye was turned (with eagerness on the part of the women and Dr. Bayard) when Miss Forrest's silken skirts came sweeping down the stairs. Her *entrée* was a triumph.

"Thought you said her neck showed her age," whispered the major to his better half. "Why, her neck and arms are superb!" a speech that cost him metaphorical salt in his coffee for the next three days. The doctor stepped forward in his most graceful manner to meet and welcome her. Captain Bruce could not refrain from hobbling up and saying a word of admiration; even Mr. Holmes fixed his dark eyes upon her in unmistakable approval, and spoke a few courteous words before he turned back to Nellie's side; and Mrs. Miller unlimbered her eye-glasses, mounted them on her prominent nose, gazed long and earnestly at the self-possessed young woman who was the centre of the group, and then looked for sympathy to Mrs. Bruce—and found it. Never in her life had Fanny Forrest looked better than she did that night. Her eyes, her color, her smiles were radiance itself; her mobile lips curved over teeth as white and gleaming as crystalled snow. Her bare neck and arms, beautifully moulded, were set off to wonderful advantage by the dress she wore,—a marvellous gown of rich, rare, lustrous black silk, that fell from her rounded hips in sweeping folds that the women could not sufficiently admire, while their eyes gloated over the wealth of gold with which the entire front from the bosom to the very hem of the skirt was heavily embroidered. An aigrette of gold shone in the dark masses of her hair, but not a vestige of gold or gems appeared either at her throat or in her ears. In her jewelled hand she carried a fan of black silk, gold embroidered like her dress, and the tiny slippers that peeped from the hem of her robe were of the same material and embroidered in a miniature of the same pattern.

"Fort Laramie never saw anything handsomer than that toilet," whispered Mrs. Bruce to the major's wife at the earliest opportunity; and the latter, kind soul, was sufficiently melted by the sight to think of her neighbors and say, "How I wish Mrs. Jordan and Mrs. Wells were here to see it!"

The dinner went off merrily as chimes a marriage-bell. The doctor was in his element when presiding at a well-appointed table; his cook was one whom he had had at Newport and Boston Harbor, and a very reliable servitor as such characters go; his wines were, some of them, gifts from wealthy and aristocratic patients whom he had managed to serve in the days when the sunshine of official favor illumined his daily life; he had a fund of anecdote and table talk; his guests were responsive and full of appreciation of the entertainment provided for them. Nellie, in her shy maidenhood, was a lovely picture at the head of his board; and Holmes, who sat at her left, was evidently more impressed than ever. A son-in-law like that, rich, manly, and educated, a leader of affairs in the city where he made his home,—the very thought lent inspiration to the doctor's life. If the judges and the senators of the East had turned their backs upon him, here he could find new power and influence among the active sons of the young and vigorous West. What a pity! What a pity! he thought, that the general commanding the division were not here. He was coming, they all knew, and might be along any day. Now, if he had only arrived in time to be one of the guests this bright evening, who can say what the effect might not have been?

It must have been just before tattoo—after they had been at the table a full hour, and tongues were loosened by the doctor's good wine, and laughter and jest and merry talk were going round—that Mrs. Miller, sitting at the doctor's right as became the lady of the commanding officer, was surprised to see the hall-door, which had been closed throughout the evening, swing very slowly a few inches inward. At the same moment the lace curtains that hung about the archway leading into the parlor swayed noiselessly toward her and then settled back to their normal position. Presently the major, who was at Miss Bayard's right, and with his back close to the hall-door, began to figdet and look uneasily about. The doctor was just telling a very good story at the moment and she could not bear to interrupt him, but after the laughter and applause had subsided she came to her husband's rescue.

"The major is keenly susceptible to colds, doctor, and I see he is fidgeting a bit. Would you mind having that door shut?"

"Which door, Mrs. Miller? Most assuredly. I thought it was closed. Here, Robert," he called to his colored servant, "go and see if the front door is shut. The wind sometimes proves too much for these quartermaster's latches," he said, apologetically. "Was it shut?" he asked, as Robert returned with an injured air as of one who had been sent on a wild-goose chase.

"Perfectly tight, sir. Ain't been open dis evenin' since Miss Forrest done got yere," was Robert's prompt reply. "I sprung de latch myself to keep it from floppin' open as it sometimes does."

"All right. Never mind. You feel no draft now, do you, major?"

"Not a particle. It was all fancy, probably." And the laughter and talk began again.

Later that long-remembered evening, as they sat around a blazing log fire, for the night had been made chilly by the rain, there was much mirth and chatter and gayety. Miss Forrest developed a new trait to make her envied. She sang with infinite spirit and a great deal of taste. Nellie's piano had known no such performer in the Western wilderness as the brilliant young woman in the lovely black silk, whose fingers went flashing over the keys, and whose voice came carolling forth in rich and wonderful notes. It was a contralto, or at least a deep mezzo, and the songs she sung were well adapted to its low and feeling tones. Mr. Holmes stood over her much of the time as she played, and applauded heartily when she had sung. "I did not expect to find such a nightingale in the wilderness," he said.

"You were looking for a very different object, were you not?" said she, raising her dark eyes to his in deep scrutiny, then dropping them quickly until the lashes swept her cheek.

"Possibly," he replied, with calm gravity. "I had several objects in view, but I rejoice in a visit that has enabled me to hear so cultured a vocalist.

I wonder no one spoke of your singing before, Miss Forrest."

"Cease to wonder, Mr. Holmes. It is the first time I have seen a piano in six months or more. We had none at Robinson, and I would have felt little like singing if there had been one."

"May I ask where you studied music?"

"You may. It is evident that, like most people I know in civilization, you are surprised to hear of accomplishments of any kind other than shooting and riding in the army."

Holmes laughed merrily. "You are loyal to the comrades of your adoption, Miss Forrest, and yet they tell me your frontier life began less than a year ago."

"True; but I like the men I've met here, and might like the women if they would let me. As yet, however, we do not seem to agree, thanks to an unfortunate propensity of mine for saying what happens to be uppermost in my mind at the moment; possibly for other good and equally sufficient reasons. You asked where I studied music? Mainly in New York and Munich."

"You have been abroad, then?"

"Years; as companion to an invalid aunt, thanks to whom I saw very little of foreign countries, and but for whom I would have seen nothing."

"You changed the subject abruptly, a moment ago, Miss Forrest. You were speaking of your relations with the ladies here. Forgive me if I refer to it, for I was interested in what you told me. Surely a woman as gifted as you are can never lack friends among her own sex. Have you never sought to win Miss Bayard, for instance?"

There was a moment's pause. Then she looked full up into his face, her fingers rippling over the keys as she spoke.

"Mr. Holmes, has it never occurred to you that in friendship, as in love, a girl of Nellie Bayard's age would prefer some one much nearer her own years?"

He drew slowly back from the piano and stood at his full height.

"The doctor is calling us to the dining-room, Miss Forrest; may I offer my arm?" was his only reply, and she arose and went with him.

They found the entire party grouped about the table, which was now decked with a great punch-bowl of beautiful workmanship. A present, the doctor explained with evident pride, from Baron Wallewski, of the Russian Legation at Washington, whom he had had the honor of pulling through a siege of insomnia two years before. It was more than anything else to display the beauty of this costly gift that he had called them once more around his board, but, since they were there, he would beg them to fill their glasses with a punch of his own composition,—"there's not a headache in a Heidelberg tun of it,"—and pledged with them the health of the distinguished donor.

A ring came at the front door as Robert was standing, tray in hand, at his master's elbow. "Say I'm engaged, if any one inquires for me," said Bayard, and launched forth into some reminiscence of the days when he and Wallewski and Bodisco and others of that ilk were at Old Point Comfort for a week together. Robert, returning from the front hall, stood in silence, like the well-trained menial he was, until his master finished his narration and the guests had sipped the toast. It was a performance of some minutes' duration, and at last the doctor turned.

"Who was it?" he said.

"Mr. McLean, sah."

"Wanted to see me."

"No, sah. The commanding officer, sah. He wouldn't come in; he's standing in the hall yet, sah. Said s'cuse him, but 'twas mos' impawtant."

Major Miller instantly set down his punch-glass, and strode out through the parlor into the front hall. It was a season of incessant rumors and alarms, and the party could not forbear listening.

"Halloo, McLean! What's up?" they heard him say.

"A courier just in from the cavalry, sir. They've had a sharp fight over in the Chug Valley, north of Hunton's. Two men killed and Lieutenant Blunt wounded. The Indians went by way of Eagle's Nest, and will try to recross the Platte below us. Captain Terry is saddling up the Grays now, and sent me to tell you. May I go with him, sir?"

"I'll be down at once. Certainly, you may go. Terry has no lieutenant for duty otherwise." The major reappeared an instant in the parlor, whither by this time all the party had hastily moved uttering exclamations of dismay and anxiety, for Blunt was a young officer beloved by every one. "You'll excuse me, doctor. I must start the troop out in pursuit at once," said Miller; and then, followed by his adjutant, he plunged forth into the darkness. When Nellie Bayard, with white cheeks, peeped timidly into the hall it was empty. McLean had gone without a look or word for her.

"By Jove, doctor, this sort of thing makes my pulses jump," exclaimed Mr. Holmes the moment the major had gone. "Can't I go and see the start? I'd like to offer a prize to the troop—or something."

"Of course you can. I'll go, too. We'll all go. I know the ladies want to. Run up and get your wraps, though it isn't raining now." And the ladies, one and all, scurried away up the stairs.

A moment later Mr. Holmes was slipping into his beaver overcoat that had been hanging in the hall. Then he began fumbling in the pockets, first one and then another. He tried the outside, then threw it open and thrust his hand into those within the broad lapels, a look of bewilderment coming over his face.

"What's the matter?" asked the doctor. "Want another cigar? Here, man! There are plenty in the dining-room; let me get you one."

"No, no! It isn't that! I've smoked enough. Wait a moment." And again he thrust his hands deep in the pockets. "Hold on till I run up to my room," he continued, and darted lightly up the stairs. The ladies were all fluttering down again and were grouped in the lower hall as he came back, laughing, but with an odd, white look about his face.

"Holmes! Something's the matter. What have you lost? What's been taken?"

"Nothing—nothing of any consequence. Come on. Let us hurry after the major, or we'll miss the fun. Mrs. Miller, permit me," and he offered his arm to the major's wife, who stood nearest the door.

"No, but I insist on knowing what is missing, Holmes. It is my right to know," called the doctor, as he struggled into his army overcoat.

"Nothing but a cigar-case and an old pocket-book. I've mislaid them somewhere and there's no time to look. Come on."

"Mr. Holmes," said Mrs. Miller in a low tone, "I have abundant reason for asking and—no! Tell me. Where was that pocket-book and how much money was there in it?"

"In my overcoat-pocket, at sunset. Probably one hundred dollars or so. I never carry much in that way. You will not speak of it, Mrs. Miller?"

"To my husband I must, and this very night. You do not dream what trouble we are in, with a thief in our very midst."

"Some of the servants, I suppose," he said, carelessly.

But to his surprise she only bowed her head and was silent a moment, then muttered rather than spoke the words,—

"God knows. I only hope so!"

V.

"WHAT a trump that young fellow McLean seems to be, doctor," said Mr. Holmes, reflectively, late that night as the two men were smoking a final cigar together.

"Oh, he's not a bad lot by any means," was the reply. "Good deal of a boy, you know. Has no experience of life. Doesn't know anything, in fact, except what professional knowledge he picked up at the Point. You can't expect anything else of an infantry subaltern whose army life has been spent out in this God-forsaken country."

"Why do you always run down this country, doctor? It's a glorious country, a magnificent country. I declare I hate the clatter and racket and rush of Chicago more and more every time I go back to it."

"That's all very well. You are unmarried, and can come and go as you please. If you were a man of family and compelled as I am to bring up a daughter in these barbaric wilds, or even to live here at all,—a man of my tastes and antecedents,—you'd curse the fates that landed you in the army. Still, I would not mind it so much if it were not for Nellie. It is galling to me to think of her having to spend so much of her fair young life in these garrison associations. Who is there here, except possibly Miss Forrest, who, by birth, education, and social position, is fit to be an intimate or friend? What opportunities has a girl of her—pardon my egotism—parentage in such a mill as this?"

Holmes almost choked over his cigar. He bent impulsively forward as though to speak, but gulped back his words, shook his head, and began puffing vigorously once more. He felt that the time had not yet come. He knew that with her he was making no progress whatever. She had been cordial, sweet, kind, as befitted her father's daughter to her father's guest; but this day, as though her woman's wit were fathoming the secret of his heart, a suspicion of reserve and distance had been creeping into her manner and deepening toward night. Then he recalled Miss Forrest's trenchant words; he remembered the white face that came back from the peep into the empty hall. Was McLean the man "nearer her own years" who had already found a lodgement in her heart? He had come back full of admiration for the young soldier whose pluck and ambition had prompted him to beg for service on a probably dangerous expedition, a pursuit of the band that had wounded his comrade and killed two of his men. He wanted to know more of him.

"Speaking of young McLean, who is he? The name is one of the best."

"Oh, he's only distantly related to the main line, I fancy. The country is full of them, but only a few belong to *the* McLeans. Of course, I suppose they all hail from the old Highland clan, but even there the line of demarcation between chieftain and gillie of the same name was broad as the border itself. If the young fellow had money or influence he'd come out well enough, provided he could travel a year or so. He needs polish, *savoir-faire*, and he can't travel because he's in debt and hasn't a penny in the world."

"How in debt? One would suppose a young fellow of his appearance could live on his pay, unless he drank or gambled. I rather fancied he wasn't given to that sort of thing."

"Oh, it isn't that; he's steady enough. The trouble with McLean is some commissary stores that were made away with by his sergeant when he was 'acting' here last winter. He could hardly help it, I suppose: the sergeant was an expert thief and hid his stealings completely, and made a very pretty penny selling bacon and flour and sugar and coffee to these Black Hills outfits going up the last year or so. When the regimental quartermaster got back and the stores were turned over to him, the sergeant promptly skipped, and McLean was found short about six hundred dollars' worth. They had a board of survey last winter, and the orders in the case were only finally issued a few weeks ago just as he returned from leave. He's got to make it all up out of his pay,—he has nothing else."

"Isn't that pretty rough on the youngster?"

"Yes, perhaps, but it's business. He won't have such confidence in human nature again. If that sergeant were back here I could account for the disappearance of your porte-monnaie by a surer hypothesis than that you lost it or dropped it. Are you sure you dropped it?"

"Well, no, I can't be sure," said Holmes, knocking the ashes off his cigar, "but it could have so happened, very easily. I was talking earnestly all the way home from the store, where we stopped coming back from stables, you remember, and I'm getting absent-minded at times. Besides, how else could it have gone, supposing it to have been in the pocket of the overcoat when I hung it in the hall just before dressing for dinner? You have had Robert years."

"He has been with me over seven years, and came to me with a high character from the old First Artillery. I never heard of his being even suspected of dishonesty."

"He is the only man who has been in the hall to-night. No one could have come in from the front while we were at dinner."

"No one without our knowledge. The door has a queer sort of latch or lock. Sometimes in high winds it would let go and blow open, but some servant who had lived here before we came put Robert up to a way of catching it that proved very effective. No; nobody was in the hall except McLean, and of course that is out of the question. Besides, he had not time. He was only there half a minute or so."

Mr. Holmes bowed without speaking. He remembered perfectly, however, that it was nearer five minutes that Mr. McLean had to wait there while the doctor was finishing that confounded story. Nevertheless, as the doctor said, that was out of the question.

"Oh, no!" he broke in hurriedly, "I cannot think any one here could have taken it. It will turn up somewhere among my other traps to-night, or else I've dropped it. Don't think of it, doctor; that distresses me far worse than the loss. Suppose we turn in now, and I'll look around my room once more."

Half an hour later the doctor tapped softly at his guest's door.

"Found it?" he asked.

"No, not yet; going to bed," was the answer, accompanied by an ostentatious yawn. "Good-night, doctor."

Mr. Holmes had indeed found no pocket-book. The discovery he made was far less welcome. An amethyst pin with sleeve-buttons to match, a piece of personal property that he highly valued, had disappeared from his dressing-case. There were three pairs of sleepless eyes in the doctor's quarters when the sentries were shouting the call of "Half-past twelve o'clock." Nellie Bayard, in her dainty little white room, was whispering over a tear-stained pillow her prayer for the safety of Randall McLean, who was riding post-haste down the swollen Platte. Dr. Bayard, too excited to go to bed, had thrown himself on a sofa and was plotting for the future and planning an alliance for his fair daughter that would mean power and position for himself. And Mr. Holmes was sitting with darkened face at his bedside, gazing blankly at the handkerchief he had picked up on the floor just in front of the bureau, a handkerchief embroidered in one corner with the letters R. McL.

* * * * * * * *

Over at the major's quarters were other sleepless eyes. It was late, nearly midnight, when the commanding officer finished dictating his telegraphic despatches to department head-quarters, and when he reached his home Mrs. Miller was still sitting up for him. A faithful and devoted spouse she was,— something of the Peggy O'Dowd order, and prone at times to order him about with scant ceremony, but quickly resentful of any slight from other sources. She could not bear that any man or woman should suppose for an instant that her major was not the embodiment of every attribute that became a soldier and a man. She stood between him and the knowledge of many a little garrison squabble or scandal rather than have him annoyed by tales that were of no consequence; but now she had that to tell that concerned the honor and welfare of the whole command, and she felt that he must know at once.

"Major," she said to him when once they had gained the seclusion of the marital chamber, "has Captain Bruce ever said anything further to you about that story from Robinson last winter?"

"N-nothing much," answered Miller, who dreaded that something more of the same kind was coming, and would gladly have avoided the subject.

"I know that he bade Mrs. Bruce destroy the letter she got and say no more about it," pursued Mrs. Miller, "but she and I are very old friends, as you know, and she could not well avoid telling me that after I told her of the letter I got. Now, it was bad enough that these things should have occurred there, and that suspicion should have attached to some one in Captain Forrest's household; but things are worse than ever now. Have you seen Mr. Hatton to-day?"

"I've seen him, of course, but he didn't say anything on—on such a subject."

"Now, I don't want you to blame Mr. Hatton, major. You must remember that he has always said that I was like a mother to him because I nursed him through the mountain fever, and he has always confided in me ever since; but the other night while he was at the Gordons', the same night he came here after tattoo, somebody went to his room and stole from his trunk over one hundred and fifty dollars in greenbacks and a beautiful scarf-pin that his brother gave him."

"And he did not report it to me?" asked the major, impetuously.

"He did not then, though he meant to, because Mr. McLean induced him to promise not to, because——"

"Well, because what? What reason could young McLean assign that could justify his concealing such a matter from the commanding officer?"

"Because he said it was cruel to allow a woman to be suspected, when she had no man in the garrison—husband, brother, or father—to take her part."

"A woman! What? some servant?"

"Worse than that, major,—Miss Forrest."

Bang! dropped the heavy boot the major had just pulled from his foot, and, one boot off and the other boot on, he started up and stood staring at his wife in blank amaze.

"Listen, dear," she said, "heaven knows it is no pleasure to tell it. She was seen, so my letter said, in the quarters of the officer who was robbed at Red Cloud, the night he was officer of the day. They lived, you know, in the same building. The night Mr. Hatton's trunk was opened she came very late to the Gordons'. Very probably it was she with whom Mr. McLean collided out on the parade, though I hushed you summarily when you began to joke about it, and Mr. Hatton hints that McLean could tell more if he would, but he has firmly set his lips against saying a word. However, that was before to-night. Now for something even worse, because it has happened to a guest within our gates. Mr. Holmes's portemonnaie with over one hundred dollars was taken from his overcoat-pocket as it hung in the hall to-night, and I saw her go out there while you were having your after-dinner smoke. I saw her go out there and stand by the hat-rack and pretend to be patting and admiring that beautiful fur. My back was turned, but the mirror over the mantel showed it."

"How do you know he lost it?"

"He told me confidentially that he was sure it was

taken from his pocket, but he is trying to make the doctor believe he lost it through his own carelessness."

"Seems to me you have confidential relations all around, Eliza; what more has been imparted to you as a secret?"

"Nothing," answered Mrs. Miller, paying no attention whatever to the first portion of the remark; "I have heard quite enough, combined with what we all know, to make me feel that either crime or kleptomania is going on, and the 'Queen of Bedlam' is at the bottom of it."

"What is it that 'we all know?'"

"That she dresses in most extravagant style; that she has suddenly had to quit her uncle's roof, where she lived for years, and come out here to be a burden on her brother, who has nothing but his pay, unless you count an invalid wife and a riotous young brood as assets. She is strange, odd, insolent, and defiant in manner. Shuns all friendship, and refuses to tell anybody what was the cause of her leaving New York as she did. One thing more,—she has sent two registered letters from here within the last three days——"

"Now, how do you know that?" burst in the major, an angry light in his eyes.

"Well, my dear, don't fly off at a tangent. It is a perfectly natural thing to speak of. Hardly anybody ever sends registered letters."

"That's not so; there are dozens sent by the officers and men after every pay-day."

"I mean hardly any women, major. I'm not talking of the men. Hardly any woman ever sends a registered letter, and so when she sent two it was not at all strange that Mrs. Griffin should speak of it to the steward's wife, and she told Mrs. Gordon's Sally, and so it came to me."

"Oh, yes. I'll be bound it reached you sooner or later," said the major wrathfully. "I'm d-blessed if anything goes on at this or any other post you women don't get hold of and knock out of shape. I shall tell Griffin that his position as postmaster won't be worth the powder to blow him into the middle of the Platte if that wife of his doesn't hold her tongue. No, I won't listen to any more of it to-night, anyway. I want to think over what you have told me."

* * * * * * * *

And over at Bedlam there were lights still burning at one o'clock. One of them shone from Mr. Hatton's room at the north end of the second floor. He was officer of the day, and that accounted for it. The other beamed from the corner window at the south, and a tall, graceful, womanly form, wrapped in a heavy shawl, was leaning against the wooden pillar on the veranda. A beautiful face was upturned to the few stars that peeped through the rifts of clouds that angrily swept the heavens. Then, as one jewelled hand clasped the railing, the other encircled the cold, white, wooden post, and in another moment the shapely head was bowed upon it, and great sobs shook the slender figure. There was the sudden rattle of an infantry sword at the other end of the piazza, and Mr. Hatton, striding forth from the hall-way, was startled to see a dim, feminine form spring from the shadows at the southern side and rush with sweeping skirts into the shelter of the Forrests' hall-way.

"I thought I heard some one crying out here," he muttered, "and supposed it was Mrs. Forrest. She's always in tears now that the captain is up in the Indian country. But who would have thought of Miss Forrest?"

VI.

AN anxious day was that that followed the departure of Captain Terry and his "grays" on their midnight ride down the Platte. The river was so high and swollen that it was certain that the Indians could have forded it only among the rocks and shoals up at Bull Bend, a day's march to the north-west, and that in getting back with their plunder to the shelter of their reservation there was only one point below Laramie where they could recross without having to swim, and that was full twenty-five miles down stream. As particulars began to come in of the fight with Blunt's little detachment the previous day, the major waxed more and more wrathful. It would seem that there were at least fifty well-armed and perfectly-mounted warriors in the party, many of them having extra ponies with them, either to carry the spoil or to serve as change-mounts when their own chargers tired. It was next to impossible that such a force should get away from the reservation without it being a matter of common talk among the old men and squaws, and so coming to the ears of the agent, whose duty it was to notify the military authorities at once.

But in this case no warning whatever had been given. The settlers in the Chugwater Valley had no signal of their coming, and two hapless "freighters," toiling up with ranch supplies from Cheyenne, were pounced upon in plain view of Hunton's, murdered and scalped and mutilated just before Blunt and his little command reached the scene. Despite the grave disparity in numbers, Blunt had galloped in to the attack, and found himself and his troopers in a hornet's nest from which nothing but his nerve and coolness had extricated them. Most of his horses were killed in the fight that followed, for Blunt promptly dismounted his men and disposed them in a circle around their wounded comrades, and thereby managed to "stand off" the Indians, despite their frequent dashes and incessant fire. After some hours of siege-work the savages had given it up and gone whooping off up the valley, and were next heard of shooting into the stage-station at Eagle's Nest. If he only had a hundred cavalry, thought Miller, he could head them off and prevent their return to the reservation, where, once they crossed the lines, they were perfectly safe and could not be touched. All told, however, Terry could only take with him some thirty men, and he was glad indeed to have McLean as a volunteer.

It was about noon when the ambulances came in

from the Chugwater, bringing Mr. Blunt and the other wounded. The assistant surgeon of the post had ridden out with them at midnight, soon after the receipt of the news; and now, while the soldiers were taken to the post hospital and comfortably established there, Mr. Blunt was carried up-stairs in the north hall of "Bedlam" and stowed away in the room opposite Hatton's. Mrs. Forrest, poor lady, nearly went into hysterics as the young soldier was lifted out of the ambulance. Day and night her soul was tortured with the dread that at any moment news might come that her husband was either killed or wounded,—and in the art of borrowing trouble she was more than an adept. Her lamentations were so loud and voluble that Miss Forrest quietly but very positively took her by the arms and marched her off the piazza into her own room, where Celestine was "trotting" the baby to sleep and nodding on the verge of a nap on her own account. The first thing Mrs. Forrest did was to whisk the half-drowsing infant out of her attendant's arms, clasp it frantically to her breast, and then go parading up and down the room weeping over the wondering little face, speedily bringing on a wailing accompaniment to her own mournful plaint. It was more than Miss Forrest could stand.

"For mercy's sake, Ruth, don't drive that baby

distracted! If you cannot control your own tears, have some consideration for the children. There!" she added, despairingly, "now you've started Maud and Vickie, and if, between the four of you, poor Mr. Blunt is not made mad by night-time, he has no nerves at all." And as she spoke the hall-way resounded with the melodious howl of the two elder children, who, coming in from play on the prairie and hearing the maternal weepings, probably thought it no less than filial on their part to swell the chorus. Miss Forrest made a rush for the door:

"Maud! Vickie! Stop this noise instantly. Don't you know poor Mr. Blunt is lying in the next hall, badly wounded and very sick?"

"Well, marmar's crying," sobbed Maud, with unanswerable logic; while Victoria, after stuttering enunciation of the words, "I'm crying because he's going to die," wound up with sudden declaration of rights by saying she didn't care whether auntie liked it or not, she'd cry all she wanted to; and, taking a fresh start, the six-year-old maiden howled afresh.

It was too much for Miss Forrest's scant patience. Seizing the little innocents in no gentle grasp, she lugged them down into the vacant dining-room on the south side of the lower hall, turned the key in the door, and bade them make themselves comfortable there until she chose to let them out. If they must howl, there was the place where they would be least likely to disturb the sufferer at the other end of the building. After which unwarrantable piece of assumption of authority she returned to her unhappy sister-in-law.

"I declare, Fanny, you have absolutely no heart at all," sobbed that lachrymose lady, as she mingled tears and sniffles with fruitless efforts to hush her infant. "Wh—what have you done with my children?"

"Shut them up in the dining-room until they stop their noises," answered Miss Forrest, calmly.

"You have no right whatever to punish my babies," indignantly protested Mrs. Forrest (and every mother will agree with her). "You are always interfering with them, and I shall write to Captain Forrest this very day and complain of it."

"I wouldn't if I were you, Ruth, because yesterday your complaint was that I never took any notice of them, no matter what they did."

"Well, you don't!" sobbed the lady of the house, abandoning the original line of attack to defend herself against this unexpected sortie. Then, suddenly recalling the more recent injury, "At least you don't when you should, and you do when you should not. Let me go to them instantly. Celestine, take baby." But Celestine had vanished.

"Give me the baby, Ruth, and go by all means. Then we can restore quiet to this side of the house at least,"—and she took with firm hands the shrieking infant from the mother's arms. Mrs. Forrest rushed down the hall and melodramatically precipitated herself upon her offspring in the dining-room. In two minutes' time the baby's wailings ceased, and when Mrs. Forrest reappeared, ready to resume the attack after having released the prisoners, she was surprised and, it must be recorded, not especially pleased to see her lately inconsolable infant laughing, crowing, and actually beaming with happiness in her sister-in-law's arms.

"I suppose you've been feeding that child sugar," she said, as she stopped short at the threshold.

"The sugar is in the dining-room, Ruth, not here."

"Well, candy, then, and you know I'd as soon you gave her poison."

"And yet you sent Celestine to my room for some for this very baby yesterday."

"I didn't!"

"Then, as I have told you more than once, Ruth, Celestine's statements are unreliable. I found her in my room, and she said you sent her for some candy for little Hal, and I gave it to her. I do not at all like her going to my room when I'm not there."

"You are down on Celestine simply because she is mine, and you know it, Fanny. It is so with everything,—everybody that is at all dear to me. That is enough to set you against them. My dear old father rescued Celestine from bondage when she was a mere baby (a favorite paraphrase of Mrs. Forrest's for describing the fact that one of that damsel's parents had officiated as cook at a Southern hospital where the chaplain happened to be on duty in the war-days). Her mother lives with his people to this hour, and she has grown up under my eyes and been my handmaiden, and the nurse of all my children, and never a word has any one ever breathed against her until you came; and you are always doing it."

"Pardon me, Ruth. I have only twice referred to what I consider her shortcomings. She was very neglectful of you and the children at Robinson, and was perpetually going out in the evening with that soldier in Captain Terry's troop, and now she is getting to be as great a gad-about here. That, however, is none of my affair, but it is my right to say that I do not want her prowling about among the trunks and boxes in my room, and if you do not exert your authority over her I must find some other means of making her respect my wishes."

"I suppose you will try and blacken her character and have her sent out of the post, and so rob us of the last relic I have of my home and f-f-friends," and Mrs. Forrest began to sob afresh.

"Hush! Ruth. I hear the doctor in the hall below. For goodness' sake, do try and look a little less like a modern Niobe when he comes up. Here, take baby," and she hugged the little fellow close and imprinted a kiss upon his dimpled cheek. "I must run down and detain him a moment until you can get straightened out."

Nothing loath was Dr. Bayard to spend some moments in *tête-à-tête* converse with Miss Forrest. She ushered him into the dining-room,—the only reception-room the two households could boast of under the stress of circumstances, and most graciously received his compliments on the "conquests" of the previous evening. "Not only all eyes, all hearts were charmed, Miss Forrest. Never even in the palmiest days of Washington society have I seen more elegant and becoming a toilet, and as for your singing,—it was simply divine." The doctor looked, as well as spoke, his well-turned phrases. He was gallant, debonair, dignified, impressive,—"a well-preserved fellow for forty-five," as he was wont to say of himself. He anxiously inquired for her health, deplored the state of anxiety and excitement in which they were compelled to live, thanked heaven that there were some consolations vouchsafed them in their exile and isolation, and begged her to be sure and send for him should she find the strain was telling upon her nervous system; it was marvellous that she should bear up so well; his little daughter was really ill this morning and unable to leave her room, but then she was a mere child. If it were not for the incomparable pleasure he—they all—found in her presence he could almost wish that Miss Forrest were once more under the shelter of her uncle's hospitable roof in New York and "free from war's alarms." By the way, where was Mr.—a—her uncle's residence?

"Mr. Courtlandt's?" she answered, promptly supplying the name. "In Thirty-fourth Street, just east of the avenue."

"To be sure; I know it well," answered the doctor. "A most refined and aristocratic neighborhood it is, and I'm sure I must have met Mr. Courtlandt at the Union Club. He is near kin, I think, to the Van Cortlandts, of Croton, is he not?"

"Not very near, doctor, though I presume there is some distant connection."

"Ah, doubtless. I recall him only vaguely. He belonged to a much older set and went very little into general society. A man of the highest social connections, however, and of much wealth." And the doctor glanced keenly at her as he propounded this tentative.

"Yes, Mr. Courtlandt is nearly sixty now, and, as you say, doctor, he goes very little into general society. He prefers his library and his books and an occasional canter in the park to any other entertainment. In fact, except his game of whist with some old cronies, that is about all the entertainment he seeks. His wife, my Aunt Laura, is quite an invalid."

"And they have no children?"

"Yes, one; a son, who is now abroad. Shall we go up and see Mrs. Forrest now, doctor? She is looking for a visit from you. Mr. Blunt's appearance was a great shock to her."

It was growing dusky as they passed through the hall-way. The sun was well down in the west, and heavy banks of rain-clouds obscured the heavens. Miss Forrest turned the knob and threw open the door leading into the unpicturesque yard at the rear of the quarters. "A little light here will be an improvement," she said. "Why! who can that be?"

As she spoke, a soldier, who had apparently been seated on the back steps, was striding hurriedly in the direction of the gate. He had started up just as she opened the door.

"Ah, my man, halt there!" called the doctor; and obediently the soldier turned and stood attention, raising his hand in salute. He was a dark, swarthy fellow, with glittering eyes and rather flat features. He wore the moustache of the trooper, and had permitted his chin whiskers to grow. The crossed sabres of the cavalry and the letter and number of the troop and regiment, all brilliantly polished, adorned his forage-cap, and his undress uniform was scrupulously neat and well-fitting. The moment he turned, Miss Forrest recognized him.

"Oh, it is Celestine's soldier friend!" she said.

"What are you doing here, my man?" asked the doctor, loftily.

"Nothing, sir," was the reply, both prompt and respectful. "The doctor probably doesn't remember me. I came in with the wounded to-day at noon,— Mr. Blunt's striker, sir."

"Well, Mr. Blunt's room is in the other division, and you ought to stay there."

"I know, sir. I've only been here a moment," was the respectful answer. "I wanted to ask Celestine to let me have a little ice if she had any, but there's no one around the kitchen."

"Go over to my quarters and tell my man Robert to give you a big lump of it. My house is yonder at the corner. Tell him Dr. Bayard sent you."

The soldier saluted, faced about, and moved away, a trifle wearily this time.

"He looks very tired," said Miss Forrest.

"I believe he is," answered the doctor. "Hold on a moment there!" he called. "Were you out with Mr. Blunt's command?"

"Yes, sir. All yesterday and last night. I had to sit up with the lieutenant all night, sir, to bathe his wound."

"True, true. And of course you hadn't a wink of sleep. Go to your barracks and get a nap. I'm going back to Mr. Blunt in five minutes, and I'll send the ice over right afterward."

"I thank the doctor, but I'm not sleepy. I'll get rest enough to-night," was the reply, and again the soldier saluted and turned away.

"How faithful and devoted those rough-looking fellows can be to their officers!" said Miss Forrest.

"Yes," answered the doctor, musingly, as he gazed after the retreating form. "Yes, very. Some of them are models,—and yet, somewhere or other I think I have seen that man before. Do you know his name?"

"No. I'll ask Celestine, if you wish to know. She ought to be up-stairs with the children now. May I not run over and see Miss Bayard presently."

"My Nellie? We shall be charmed. If you will only wait a moment until I have seen Mr. Blunt, I shall be delighted to escort you. She is all alone unless Mrs. Miller has returned to her, and the house is deserted down-stairs. Mr. Holmes is out somewhere with the major."

But Miss Forrest did not wait. No sooner had the doctor finished his brief visit to her sister-in-law than the young lady threw a light wrap over her shoulders, and, just as the bugle was sounding first call for retreat, she walked rapidly to the big house at the south-west corner, noiselessly opened the door without the formality of ringing for admission, and in the gathering darkness of the hall-way within, where she had to grope a moment to find the banister-rail, she came face to face with Mrs. Miller.

VII.

Cold and still the dawn is breaking. Faint, wan, and pallid is the feeble gleam that comes peeping over the low hills far over at the east. Bare and desolate look the barren slopes on every hand. Not a tree, not a shrub of any kind can eye discover in this dim and ghostly light. All is silence, too. Even the coyotes who have set up their unearthly yelping at odd intervals during the night seem to have slunk away before the coming of the morning's sun and sought the shelter of their lurking-spots. Here on the bleak ridge, where three men, wrapped in cavalry overcoats, are lying prone, not a sound of any kind beyond an occasional muffled word is to be heard. Three hundred yards behind them, down in the valley, some thirty shadowy steeds are cropping at the dense buffalo-grass, while their riders, dismounted now, are huddled together for warmth. The occasional stamp of a hoof and the snort of some impatient charger break the silence here, but cannot be heard out at the front where the picket is lying. Another sound, soothing, monotonous, ceaseless, falls constantly upon the ear of the waking soldiers,—the rush of the swollen Platte over the rocks and gravel of the ford a quarter-mile away, the only point below the fort where the renegade Sioux can recross without swimming, and they are not yet here to try it. When they come they will find Captain Terry, with young McLean and thirty troopers, lurking behind the covering ridge, ready and willing to dispute the passage. Through the darkness of the night those good gray steeds, flitting like ghosts along the shore, have come speeding down the Platte to land their riders first at the goal, and once here, and satisfied by scrutiny of the south entrance to the ford that no Indian pony has appeared within the last twenty-four hours, Terry has posted his lookouts on the ridge, and then, having hoppled and "half-lariated" his horses, has cautioned the men to rest on their arms and not to throw off belt or spur. "There is no telling," he says, "what moment they may come along."

McLean, with his long Springfield rifle, has gone up to the ridge to join the outlying picket. A keen-eyed fellow is this young soldier and a splendid shot, and the Indians who succeed in crossing that next ridge a mile farther south and approaching them unobserved will have to wear the cap of the "Invisible Prince." He has come out on this scout full of purpose and ambition. Things have not gone happily with him during the past few days. Profoundly depressed in spirits at the millstone of debt suddenly saddled upon him as the result of peculations of the deserting sergeant, he has the added misery of seeing the sweet-faced girl with whom he has fallen so deeply in love practically withdrawn from his daily life and penned up within her father's house for the evident object of compelling her to entertain the devotion of a rival, whose wealth and social position make him a man to be feared,—a man whom any woman, old or young, might think twice before refusing. Already the people at Laramie were discussing the possibilities,—some of them in his very presence; and there were not lacking those to say, that, even if she had been more than half inclined to reciprocate McLean's evident attachment, she would be a fool not to accept Roswell Holmes, with his wealth, education, and undoubted high character. A second lieutenant in the army was all very well for a girl who could do no better, but Elinor Bayard was of excellent social position herself. Her mother's people ranked with the best in the land, and her father, despite his *galanterie*, was a man distinguished in his profession and in society. It was driving McLean wellnigh desperate. Not one word of love-making had been breathed between him and the gentle girl who so enjoyed her walks and rides with him, but he knew well that her woman's heart must have told her ere this how dear she was to him, and it was no egotism or conceit that prompted him to the belief that she would not show such pleasure in his coming if he were utterly indifferent to her. Coquetry was something Nellie Bayard seemed deficient in; she was frank and truthful in every look and word.

And yet, realizing what grounds he had for hope, McLean was utterly downcast when he faced the situation before him. It would take him a year— with the utmost economy he could command—to pay off the load that had been so ruthlessly heaped upon him. He realized that so long as he owed a penny in the world he had no right to ask any woman to be his wife. Meantime, here was this wealthy, well-educated, well-preserved man of affairs ready and eager to lay his name and fortune at her feet. What mattered it that he was probably more than double her age? Had McLean not read of maidens who worshipped men of more than twice their years even to the extent of—"A love that was her doom?" Had he not read aloud to her only a fortnight before the story of Launcelot and the lily maid of Astolat? Poor fellow! In bitterness of spirit he believed that in the last few days she had purposely avoided him, and had treated him with coldness on the few occasions when they met; and now he had sought this perilous duty eagerly and avowedly; he had set forth without so much as a word of farewell to her or a touch of her trembling little hand, affecting to be so occupied in preparation up to the instant of starting that he had no time for a word with anybody. And yet Mrs. Miller had called him aside and spoken to him as the group of officers and ladies gathered near the Laramie bridge to see the little column start, and Nellie Bayard had looked up wistfully at him as he rode by their party, merely waving his scouting-hat in general salutation. It hurt her sorely that he should have gone without one word for her,—and yet she scarce knew why.

And now here they were, squarely across the Indian trail, and ready for their coming. Roswell Holmes could not have that distinction at all events, thought McLean, as he tried the lock and breech-block of his rifle to see that everything was in perfect working order. Come what might,—if it were only Indians,—he meant to make a record in this fight that any woman might be proud of; and if he fell, —well, he wouldn't have to pay for Sergeant Marsland's stealings, or have the misery of seeing her borne off by Holmes's big bank-account, as she probably would be. Poor Mac! He had yet to learn that a reputation as an Indian-fighter is but an ephemeral and unsatisfactory asset as an adjunct to love-making.

Meanwhile, the dawn is broadening; the grayish pallor at the orient takes on a warmer tint, and a feeble glow of orange and crimson steals up the heavens. The slopes and swales around the lonely outpost grow more and more visible, the distant ridge more sharply defined against the southern sky. Off to the left, the eastward, the river rolls along in a silvery, misty gleam; and their comrades, still sheltered under the bluff, are beginning to gather around the horses and look to the bridles and "cinchas." Now the red blush deepens and extends along the low hill-tops across the Platte, and tinges the rolling prairie to the south and west. A few minutes more and the glow is strong enough to reveal an old but well-defined trail leading from the distant ridge straight up to the little crest where McLean is lying. It seems to follow a south-westerly course, and is the trail, beyond doubt, along which the marauders from the reservations have time and again recrossed with their plunder and gained the official shelter of those sacred limits.

"Why, sir," says Corporal Connor, who is lying there beside the young officer, "last October a party came over and scalped two women and three teamsters not three miles from the post, and ran off with all their cattle. We caught up with them just across the Niobrara, and they dropped the mules and horses they were driving and made a run for it. We chased and gained on them every inch of the way, but they got to the lines first, and then they just whirled about and jeered at us and shook the scalps in our faces, and called us every name you could think of,—in good English, too," added the trooper seriously; "and the lieutenant and I rode to the agency and pointed out two of them to the agent that very day, but he didn't dare arrest them. His life depended on his standing by them through thick and thin. Look, lieutenant! Look off there!"

Over to the southwest, dimly visible, three or four shadowy objects are darting rapidly over the distant ridge that spans the horizon in that direction. For one moment only they are revealed against the sky, then can be seen, faint as far-away cloud-shadows, sweeping down into the shallow valley and making for the river above the position of the outpost. Indians, beyond question! the advance guard of the main body; and the time for action has come.

Instead of riding toward them, however,—instead of approaching the ford by the most direct line,— these scouts are loping northward from the point where the trail crosses the ridge, and pushing for the stream. McLean sees their object with the quickness of thought. 'Tis not that they have made a "dry camp" during the night, and are in haste to get to water with their ponies. He knows well that in several of the ravines and "coulies" on their line of march there is abundant water at this season of the year. He knows well that not until they had crept up to and cautiously peered over that ridge, without showing so much as a feather of their warbonnets, would they venture so boldly down into the "swale." He knows well that both in front and rear they are watching for the coming of cavalry, and that now they are dashing over to the Platte to peer across the skirting bluffs until satisfied no foeman is near, then to scurry down into the bottom to search for hoof-prints. If they find the well-known trail of shod horses in column of twos, it will tell them beyond shadow of doubt that troops are already guarding the ford. "Confound it!" he exclaims. "Why didn't we think of it last night, and come down the other side? We could just as well have crossed the Platte on the engineer bridge, and then they couldn't have spotted us. Now it's too late. Run back, corporal, and warn the captain. I'll stay here and watch them."

Connor speeds briskly down the slope, and, even as they see him coming, the men lead their horses into line. Captain Terry has one foot in the stirrup as the non-commissioned officer reaches him and his hand goes up in salute.

"Lieutenant McLean's compliments, sir" (the invariable formula in garrison, and not omitted in the field by soldiers as precise as the corporal). "Three or four bucks are galloping over to the river above us to look for our tracks."

"How far above us, corporal?"

"Nigh on to a mile, sir."

"Sergeant Wallace, stay here with the platoon. Mount, you six men on the right, and come after me as quick as you can!" And away goes Captain Terry, full speed up the valley and heading close under the bluffs. In a minute three of the designated troopers are in a bunch at his heels, the other three scattered along the trail. From McLean's post he can see both parties in the gathering light,—the Indians, slowly and cautiously now, beginning the ascent to the bluffs, the captain and his men "speeding it" to get first to the scene. Another moment, and he sees Terry spring from his horse, throw the reins to a trooper, and run crouching up toward the crest; then, on hands and knees, peep cautiously over, removing his hat as he does so. Then he signals "forward" to his men, slides backward a yard or two, runs to his horse, mounts, gallops some four hundred yards farther along the foot of the slope, then turns, rides half-way up, and then he and four of the men leap from their saddles, toss their reins to the two who remain mounted, and, carbine in hand, run nimbly up the bluffs and throw themselves prone upon the turf, almost at the top. Not two hundred yards away from them four Sioux warriors, with trailing war-bonnets and brilliant display of paint and glitter, are "opening out" as they approach, and warily moving toward the summit. One instant more and there is a sudden flash of fire-arms at the crest; five jets of bluish smoke puff out upon the rising breeze; five sputtering reports come sailing down the wind a few seconds later; and, while two of the warriors go whirling off in a wide, sweeping circle, the other two are victims to their own unusual recklessness. One of them, clinging desperately to the high pommel, but reeling in his saddle, urges his willing pony down the slope; the other has plunged forward and lies stone-dead upon the sward. Even at the echo of the carbines, however, popping up from across the ridge a mile away, there come whirling into view a score of red and glittering horsemen, sweeping down in broad, fan-shaped course, at top speed of their racing ponies, yelling like mad, and lashing their nimble steeds to the rescue. Two minutes of that gait, and the captain and his little squad will be surrounded.

"Mount! mount!" shouts McLean, as he turns and rushes down the slope, followed by his picket-guard. "Lively now, sergeant. Run to the captain. Don't wait for me!"

"Come on, all you fellers!" is Sergeant Wallace's characteristic rallying cry; and away goes the little troop, like a flock of quail. McLean is in the saddle in an instant, and full tilt in pursuit.

Not a moment too soon! Even before the leading troopers have reached the two "horse-holders" under the bluffs, both above and below the captain's position, the plumed and painted warriors have flashed up on the ridge and taken him in flank. Without the prompt aid of his men he would be surrounded in the twinkling of an eye. Already these daring flankers have opened fire on the knot of horsemen, when Mc-Lean shouts to some of the rearmost to follow him, and veering to the left he rides straight at the Indians who have appeared nearest him along the bluffs. Two of the troopers follow unhesitatingly; others sheer off toward their main body. There's too much risk in darting right into the teeth of a pack of mounted Sioux, even to follow an officer. Wary and watchful the Indians mark his coming. Circling out to right and left they propose to let him in, then follow their old tactics of a surround. He never heeds their manœuvres; his aim is to get to close quarters with any one of them and fight it out, as Highland chieftains fought in the old, old days of target and claymore.

He never heeds the whistle of the bullets past his ears as one after another the nearest Indians take hurried shots at him. Straight as a dart he flies at a tall savage who pops up on the ridge in front of him. The long Springfield is slung now, and he grasps the gleaming revolver in his hand. Twice the Indian fires, the lever of his Henry rifle working like mad, but the bullets whiz harmlessly by; then, with no time to reload, and dreading the coming shock, he ducks quickly over his nimble piebald's neck and strives to lash him out of the way, just as the young officer from some other hand

Receives but recks not of a wound,

and then troop-horse, pony, soldier, and savage are rolling in a confused heap upon the turf. The Indian is the first on his feet and limping away; no redskin willingly faces white man "steel to steel." McLean staggers painfully to his knees, brushes dust and clods from his blinded eyes with one quick dash of his sleeve, and draws a bead on his red antagonist just as the latter turns to aim; there is a sudden flash and report, and the Sioux throws up his hands with one yell and tumbles headlong. Then a mist seems rising before the young soldier's eyes, the earth begins to reel and swim and whirl, and then all grows dark, and he, too, is prostrate on the sward.

VIII.

THEY were having an anxious day of it at Laramie. Early in the morning a brace of ranchmen, still a-tremble from their experiences of the night, made their way into the post and told gruesome stories of the doings of the Indians at Eagle's Nest and beyond. The Cheyenne stage, they said, was "jumped," the driver killed, and the load of passengers burned alive in the vehicle itself. There might have been only fifty warriors when they fought Lieutenant Blunt and his party in the Chug Valley, but they must have been heavily re-enforced, for there were two hundred of them at the least count when they swept down upon the little party of heroes at the stage station. They fought them like tigers, said the ranchmen, but they would probably have burned the building over their heads and "roasted the whole outfit" had it not been that the coming of the stage had diverted their attention. These were the stories with which the two worthies had entertained the guard and other early risers pending the appearance of the commanding officer; and these were the stories that, in added horrors and embellishments, spread throughout the garrison, through kitchen to breakfast-room, as the little community began to make its appearance down-stairs. Major Miller, a veteran on the frontier, had taken the measure of his informants in a very brief interview. Aroused by the summons of Lieutenant Hatton, to whom as officer of the day the guard had first conducted these harbingers of woe, the major had shuffled down-stairs in shooting-jacket and slippers, and cross-examined them in his dining-room. Both men looked wistfully at the brimming decanter on his sideboard, and one of them "allowed" he never felt so used up in his life; so the kind-hearted post commander lugged forth a demijohn and poured out two stiff noggins of whiskey, refreshed by which they retold their tale. Miller "gave them the rein" for five minutes and then cross-questioned, as a result of which proceeding he soon dismissed them to the barracks and breakfast, and announced to Hatton and the adjutant that there would be no change in the orders,—he didn't believe one-fourth of their story. The stage, he said, wasn't due at Eagle's Nest until four o'clock in the morning, and these men had declared it burned at three. It was utterly improbable that it came farther than Phillips's crossing of the Chugwater, where it was due at midnight, and where long before that time all the hands at the station had been warned, both by couriers and fugitives, that the Indians were swarming up the valley. They had cut the telegraph-wire, of course, on striking the road, early in the afternoon, and it was impossible to tell just how things had been going; but he was willing to bet that the stage was safe, despite the assertions of the ranchmen that they had seen the blaze and heard the appalling shrieks of the victims. The major's confidence, however, could not be shared by the dozen houses full of women and children whose closest protectors were far away on the fields where duty called them. Laramie was filled with white, horror-stricken faces and anxious eyes, as the ladies flitted from door to door before the call for guard-mounting, and "boomed" the panic-stricken ranchmen's story until it reached the proportions of a wholesale massacre and an immediately impending siege of the fort by Red Cloud and all his band. Women recalled the fearful scene at Fort Phil Kearney in 1866, when the same old chieftain, Mach-pe-a-lo-ta, surrounded with a thousand warriors the little detachment of three companies and butchered them within rifle range of the trembling wives and children at the post; and so by the time the story reached the doctor's kitchen it had assumed the dimensions of a colossal tragedy. They were just gathering in the breakfast-room,—Nellie a trifle pale and weary-looking, the doctor and Holmes a bit the worse for having sat up so late and smoked so many cigars, but disposed to be jovial and youthful for all that. Coffee was not on the table, and Robert failed to respond to the tinkling of the little silver bell. Then sounds of woe and lamentation were heard in the rear, and the doctor impatiently strode to the door and shouted for his domestics. Robert responded, his kinky wool bristling as though electrified and his eyes fairly starting from their sockets; he was trembling from head to foot.

"What's the matter, you rascal, and why do you not answer the bell?" angrily demanded his master.

But it was "the Johnsons' Winnie" who responded. She had doubtless been going the rounds, and was only waiting for another chance to make a dramatic *coup*. Rushing through the kitchen, she precipitated herself into the breakfast-room. "Oh, Miss Nellie," she sobbed, "there's drefful news. The Indians burned the stage with everybody in it, and they've shot Captain Terry and Mr. McLean an' all the soldiers with 'em, an'——"

"Silence, you babbling idiot!" shouted Dr. Bayard. "Stop your fool stories, or I'll——"

"But it's God's truth, doctor. It's God's truth," protested Winnie, desperately determined to be defrauded of no part of her morning's sensation. "Ask anybody. Ask the sergeant of the guard. Yo' can see the men what brought the news yo'self."

"Pardon me, doctor," interrupted Mr. Holmes, in

calm, quiet tones. "This has been too much of a shock for Miss Bayard, I fear." And already he was by her side, holding a glass of water to her pallid lips. The doctor pointed to the door.

"Leave the room, you pestilence in petticoats!" he ordered. "Go!" And, having accomplished her desire to create a sensation, though balked of the full fruition of the promised enjoyment, Winnie flew to "Bedlam," where she only prayed that Celestine might not be before her with the news. Meantime, Dr. Bayard had turned to his daughter. His first impulse was to reprove her for her ready credence of the story set afloat by so notorious a gabbler as the Johnsons' "second girl." One glance at Elinor's pale features and drooping mien changed his disposition in a trice. Anxiously he stepped to her side, and his practised hand was at her pulse before a word of question was uttered. Then he gently raised her head.

"Look up, daughter! Why, my little girl, this will never do! I don't believe a word of this absurd story, and you must not let yourself be alarmed by such fanciful pictures. Come, dear! Mr. Holmes will excuse you this morning. Let me get you to your room. Will you kindly touch that bell, Holmes, and send Chloe to me? I'll rejoin you in a moment. Come, Nell?"

And half leading, half carrying, he guided her from the room and up the stairs, while Holmes, with grave and thoughtful face, stood gazing after them. It was some time before the doctor reappeared, even after Chloe joined him in the chamber of her young mistress. When he did the breakfast was cold, and both men were too anxious to get the true story to care whether they breakfasted or not. Each took a swallow of coffee, then hastened forth.

"That poor little girl of mine!" said Dr. Bayard. "She has a very nervous, sensitive organization, and such a shock as that fool of a wench gave her this morning is apt to upset her completely. Now, she has no especial interest in any of Terry's party, and yet you might suppose her own kith and kin had been scalped and tortured."

But Holmes would not reply.

Meantime, Winnie had reached "Bedlam," where, to her disgust, Celestine had already broached the tidings to the breakfast-table, and Mrs. Forrest had been borne half fainting to her room. Pale, but calm and collected, Miss Forrest returned and began questioning the girl as to the sources of her information, and it was on hearing this colloquy that Winnie took heart of grace and impulsively sprang up the steps into the hall-way to add her share to the general sensation. It was with a feeling bordering on exultation that she found the local account to be lacking in several of the most startling and dramatic particulars. Celestine had not heard of the massacre of Captain Terry's command, and it was her own proud privilege to break the news to Miss Forrest. Here, however, she overshot the mark, for that young lady looked determinedly incredulous, dismissed her colored informant as no longer worthy of consideration, and, taking a light wrap from the hat-rack in the hall, tapped at Mrs. Post's door.

"Will you kindly look after Mrs. Forrest a moment in case she should need anything? I will go to Major Miller's and investigate these stories. They seem absurd."

And with that she sped swiftly around the parade, along the broad walk, and was quickly at the major's door and ushered into the parlor. There were Dr. Bayard and Mr. Holmes in earnest talk with the commanding officer. All three arose and greeted her with marked courtesy.

"I am sorry that my wife is not here to welcome you, Miss Forrest," said the major, "but with the exception of her and yourself the entire feminine element of this garrison is stampeded this morning; the women have frightened themselves out of their senses. Have you come for Dr. Bayard? I hope Mrs. Forrest has not collapsed, as Mrs. Gordon has.

Mrs. Miller has gone to pull her out of a fit of hysterics."

"Mrs. Forrest will need nothing more, I think, than an assurance that there is little truth in these stories."

"Upon my word, Miss Forrest, I believe they are as groundless as—other sensational yarns that have come to my ears. Two badly-scared ranchmen are responsible for kindling the fire, but the nurse-maids and cooks have fanned it into a Chicago conflagration. The Indians may have built a fire down the road beyond Eagle's Nest, but I'll bet it wasn't the stage. And as for Terry and McLean, we haven't a word of any kind from them. That story is built out of wind."

"Then will you pardon me, Dr. Bayard, if I suggest that it might be well if some one in authority were to warn the hospital nurse who is with Mr. Blunt, to be sure and let no one approach him with such news as has been flying around the post? I fear he had a restless night."

"A most thoughtful suggestion, my dear young lady, and, if you are going home, I will escort you, and then go to Blunt at once. May I have that pleasure?"

"I—had hoped to see Mrs. Miller, doctor, and think I will go to the east side a moment and inquire for Mrs. Gordon."

"By all means, Miss Forrest, and so will I," answered Bayard, bowing magnificently. "You will excuse me, Mr. Holmes? I will be home in a quarter of an hour."

"Certainly, doctor, certainly," was the prompt reply, and both Major Miller and Mr. Holmes followed the two out upon the piazza and stood watching them as they walked away.

"A singularly handsome and self-possessed young woman that, Mr. Holmes!" remarked the major. "Now, there's the sort of girl to marry in the army. She has nerve and courage and brains. By Jove! That's one reason, I suppose, the women don't like her!"

"And they do not like her?" queried Holmes.

"Can't bear her, I judge, from what I hear. She dresses so handsomely, they say, that she's an object of boundless interest to them,—like or no like."

"Our friend the doctor seems decidedly an ardent admirer. He was showing himself off in most brilliant colors last night, and evidently for her benefit."

"Oh, yes, I rather fancied as much. They would make a very distinguished couple," said the colonel, reflectively, "and no bad match, despite the disparity in years. She refused two youngsters up at Red Cloud who were ready to cut each other's throats on her account. That's one reason I admire her sense.

The idea of a woman like that, or any woman, marrying a second lieutenant!"

"You waited for your 'double bars,' major?" smilingly queried Mr. Holmes.

"Oh, Lord, no!" laughed Miller. "Like most people who preach, I'm past the practising age. I was married on my graduation leave,—but things were different before the war. Army people didn't live in the style they put on now. Our wives were content with two rooms and a kitchen, a thousand a year, and one new dress at Christmas. Now!" but the major stopped short, words failing him in the contemplation of mightiness as shown in the contrast.

"I'm no great judge of women," said Holmes, presently, "but that young lady roused my interest last night. Are there any tangible reasons why they should give her the cold shoulder?"

Miller colored in the effort to appear at ease.

"None that I have any personal knowledge of or feel like treating with respect. There's no accounting for women's whims," he added, sententiously. "Jupiter! Here it is nine o'clock, and nothing done yet. I can't telegraph, for they've cut the wires. I've sent out scouts, but it may be noon before they'll get back. Meantime, we have to sit here with our hands tied, and the devil to pay generally in garrison. Ah! there go the doctor and Miss Forrest over to 'Bedlam.' Isn't he a magnificent old cock? Just see him court her! Will you come with me to the office?"

"I believe not, major. I think I'll walk around a little. I'm a trifle fidgety myself this morning, and eager for reliable news. There's no objection, is there, to my going down to the barracks and interviewing those ranchmen? You know I'm something of a 'cow-puncher' myself, and may be able to squeeze some grain of truth out of them."

"No, indeed! Go ahead, Mr. Holmes, and if you extract anything veritable let me know."

Passing Bedlam, Mr. Holmes glanced up at the open gallery where the hospital attendant happened to be standing. The doctor had entered the other hall with Miss Forrest, and was doubtless majestically ministering to the nervous ailments of her sister-in-law.

"How is Lieutenant Blunt this morning?" he asked.

"He had a hard night, sir," was the low-toned answer. "He was in a high fever much of the time, but he seems sleeping now. Is there any further news, Mr. Holmes?"

"There is no truth in the news you have heard, if you have been afflicted with the stories sent around the post this morning. Be sure and keep everything of the kind from Mr. Blunt. Here! Can you catch?" And fumbling in his waistcoat-pocket, he fetched out a glittering gold piece and tossed it deftly to the gallery. It fell upon the boards with a musical ring, and was quickly pounced upon by the man, who blushed and grinned awkwardly.

"I don't like to take this, sir," he said. "It's five dollars."

"Never mind what it is! It's worth a thousand times its weight if you keep all such yarns from the lieutenant.—Oh! Good-morning, Mr. Hatton! I thought your rooms were up-stairs," he said, as at that moment the infantryman stepped forth from the lower hall.

"They are, Mr. Holmes, but I have taken up my quarters temporarily in McLean's, so as not to disturb Blunt with the creaking of those ramshackle old stairs. What is Mac's is mine, and *vice versa*. Won't you come in?"

Mr. Holmes hesitated a moment. Then a sudden thought struck him. He sprang lightly up the steps and was ushered into the sanctum of the young soldier, whom he had marked the night before starting upon the scout with Terry's troopers.

"So this is McLean's vine and fig-tree, is it?" said he, as he looked curiously around. "Ha! Lynchburg sun-dried, golden leaf! Can I have a pipe?"

"Most assuredly! Excuse me five minutes, while I run over to the guard-house. Then I'll rejoin you, and we'll have a whiff together." Another moment, and Mr. Holmes was sole occupant of the premises.

He seemed to forget his desire for a smoke, and in its stead to become possessed with a devil of mild inquisitiveness. After a rapid glance around the front room, with its bare, barrack-like, soldier furnishing, he stepped quickly into the bed-chamber in the rear and went unhesitatingly to the bureau. The upper drawer came out grudgingly and with much jar and friction, as the drawers of frontier furniture are apt to do even at their best, but his firm hand speedily reduced it to subjection. A little pile of handkerchiefs, neatly folded, stood in the left-hand corner. He lifted the topmost, carried it to the window, compared the embroidered initials with those of the handkerchief he took from an inside pocket, scribbled a few closely-written words on a blank card, carefully folded the handkerchief he had brought with him, slipped the card inside the folds, replaced both on the pile, closed the drawer, and was placidly puffing away at his pipe when Hatton returned.

IX.

LATE that afternoon the guard caught sight of a horseman loping rapidly up the valley and heading for the bridge across the Laramie. Long before he reached the post an orderly had notified the commanding officer that a courier was coming,—doubtless from Captain Terry's party, and Major Miller's appearance on his north piazza, binocular in hand, and gazing steadfastly over the distant flats to the winding trail along the river, was sufficient to bring strong representations of every household into view, all eager to see what he was seeing or to hear what he might know. Mr. Hatton came hurriedly over from "Bedlam," took his place by the major's side, and a peep through the same big glasses. Then, after a moment's consultation, the two officers started down the steps and walked briskly past the quarters on the east side, merely calling, in answer to the many queries, "Somebody coming with news from Terry!" and by the time they reached the old blockhouse at the north end, the somebody was in plain view, urging his foam-flecked and panting steed to a plunging gallop as he neared the Laramie. The hoofs thundered across the rickety wooden bridge, and the rider was hailed by dozens of shrill and wailing voices as he passed the laundresses' quarters, where the whole population had turned out to demand information. The adjutant had joined the commanding officer by this time, and several of the guard had come forth, anxious and eager to hear the news. No man in the group could catch the reply of the horseman to the questioners at "Sudstown," but in an instant an Irish wail burst upon the ear, and, just as one coyote will start a whole pack, just as one midnight bray will set in discordant chorus a whole "corral" of mules, so did that one wail of mourning call forth an echoing "keen" from every Hibernian hovel in all the little settlement, and in an instant the air rang with unearthly lamentations.

"D—— those absurd women!" growled the major, fiercely, though his cheek paled at dread of the coming tidings. "They'll have all the garrison in hysterics. Here, Hatton! run down there and stop their infernal noise. There isn't one in a dozen of 'em that has any idea of what has happened. They're howling on general principles. What the devil does that man mean by telling his news before he sees the commanding officer, anyhow?"

Meantime, straight across the sandy flats and up the slope came the courier, his horse panting loudly.

Half-way from "Sudstown" he was easily recognized,—Corporal Zook, of "Terry's Grays," and a tip-top soldier. Reining in his horse, throwing the brown carbine over his shoulder and quickly dismounting, he stepped forward to the group and, with the unfailing salute, handed his commander a letter.

"How came you to tell those women anything?" asked Miller, his lips and hands trembling slightly, despite his effort to be calmly prepared for the worst. "Don't you see you've started the whole pack of them to yowling? I thought I warned you never to do that again, when you came in with the news of Lieutenant Robinson's murder."

"The major did, sir; I had it in mind when I came in sight of those Irishwomen this time, and wouldn't open my lips, sir. They are bound to make a row, whatever happens. I only shook my head at them, sir." And Corporal Zook, despite fatigue, hard riding, and dust, appeared, if one could judge by a slight twinkle of the eye, to take a rather humorous view of this exposition of national traits. Followed by two or three of the guard, Mr. Hatton had obediently hastened to quell the tumult of lamentation, but by the time he reached the nearest shanty the infection had spread throughout the entire community, and—women and children alike—the whole populace was weeping, wailing, and gnashing its teeth,—and no one knew or cared to know exactly why. Having been wrought up to a pitch of excitement by the rumors and rapid moves of the past forty-eight hours, nothing short of a massacre could now quite satisfy Sudstown's lust for the sensational, and, defrauded of the actual cause for universal bewailing, was none the less determined to indulge in the full effect. Poor Hatton had more than half an hour of stubborn and troublesome work before he could begin to quell the racket in the crowded tenements, and meantime there was mischief to pay in the fort. No sooner did the Irish wail come floating on the wind than the direst rumors were rushed from house to house. The courier had barely had time to hand his despatches to Major Miller, and the major had not had time to read them, when a messenger came post-haste for Dr. Bayard, and stood trembling and breathless at his door while the punctilious old major-domo went to call his master. Holmes was reading at the moment in the doctor's library, and, at the sound of excited voices and scurrying footfalls without, came forward into the hall just as the door of Nellie's room was heard to open. Glancing up, he caught sight of her at the head of the stairs,—her hair dishevelled and rippling down over her shoulders and nearly covering the dainty wrapper she wore.

"Mr. Holmes! please see what has happened?" she cried, with wild anxiety in her eyes. "I hear such dreadful noise, and see men running down toward the laundresses' quarters."

But there was no need for him to ask. The messenger at the door was only too eager.

"Oh, Miss Nellie!" she called, sobbing, half in eagerness, half in genuine distress. "There's such dreadful news! There's a man come in from Captain Terry's troop, and they've had a terrible fight, and Mr. McLean an' lots of 'em are killed. It's all true, just as we heard it this——"

But here Mr. Holmes slammed the door in the foolish creature's face and went tearing up the stairs, four at a bound, for, clasping the balusters with both her little hands in a grasp that seemed loosening every second, Nellie Bayard was sinking almost senseless to the floor. Chloe, too, came running to her aid, and, between them, they bore her to the sofa in her pretty room, and then the doctor reached them, almost rejoicing to find her in tears, instead of the dead faint he dreaded.

"How could I have been so mad as to bring her to such a pandemonium as this?" was his exclamation to Holmes as, a moment later, they hastened forth upon the parade. "Yes," he hastily answered, as a little boy came running tearfully to him, to say that mamma was taken very ill and they didn't know what to do for her. "Yes. So are all the women in garrison, I doubt not; though they're all scared for nothing, I'll bet a dinner. Tell mamma I'll be there just as soon as I've seen Major Miller. Here he comes now."

The major, with his adjutant, and followed by his orderly, was coming rapidly into the quadrangle as he spoke, and the two gentlemen hastened forward to meet him. From half a dozen houses women or children were rushing to question the commanding officer with wild, imploring eyes and faltering tongues. He waved his hands and arms in energetic gyrations and warned them away.

"Go back! Go back! You distracted geese!" he called. "It's all a lie! There's hardly been a brush worth mentioning. Terry and his men are all safe. Now, do stop your nonsense! But come with me, doctor," he quickly added, in a lower tone. "Come, Mr. Holmes. I want you both to hear this. It's so like Terry. D—— those outrageous Bridgets down there! Did you ever hear anything like the row they raised? And all for nothing."

"Has there been no fight at all?" asked Dr. Bayard.

"Yes,—a pretty lively one, too. McLean is shot and otherwise hurt, but can't be dangerously so, for he wanted to go on in the pursuit. Three horses killed and two troopers wounded; that's about the size of it, but there's more to come. Doctor, I want two ambulances to go down at once, and will send half a dozen men as guard. They can ride in them. We have no more available troopers. Will you go or send your assistant? You cannot get there much before ten or eleven o'clock, even if you trot all the way. Better let Dr. Weeks go, don't you think so?"

"Whichever you prefer, major. Weeks has been devoting himself to Blunt, though of course I could relieve him there. When could we get back?"

"Not before noon to-morrow. The wounded are 'way down at Royal's Ford, where Terry had left them with two or three men, and pushed on after the Indians with the rest. They tricked him, I fancy, and he isn't in good humor."

By this time the quartet had entered the office, and there, handing the despatch to his adjutant, and bidding the orderly close the door, the major seated himself at his desk; invited the others to draw up their chairs; produced a map of the Platte country and the trails to the Sioux Reservation over along the White River, and bade the adjutant read aloud. This the young officer proceeded to do:

"On the Trail, near Niobrara, 10.30 a.m.

"Post Adjutant, Fort Laramie:

"Sir,—Reaching Royal's Ford before daybreak, we posted lookouts and headed off the Indians, who appeared at dawn. In the fight Lieutenant McLean, Sergeant Pierce, and Trooper Murray were wounded; two Indians killed and left on the field; others wounded, but carried off. After skirmishing some time at long range, they drew off, and were next seen far down the Platte below the ford. I started at once in pursuit, but had gone only four miles when we discovered it was only a small band, and that the main body, with considerable plunder, had got down to and were crossing the ford. This led us to hasten back, and we have kept up hot pursuit to this point. Now, however, the horses are exhausted, and we have not even gained upon their fresh ponies, although they were forced to abandon a good many horses they were driving away. As soon as our horses and men are rested, I will start on return *via* the north bank. Please send ambulance, etc., for the wounded.

"Very respectfully, your obedient servant,
"George F. Terry,
"*Captain Commanding.*"

To this military and matter-of-fact correspondence the auditors listened in silence.

"Not much about that to stir up such a bobbery!" said the major, presently.

"How did you hear about McLean's wanting to join the pursuit?" inquired Mr. Holmes. "Captain Terry seems to make rather slight mention of him and the other wounded. I know enough of Indian-fighting to feel sure there must have been some sharp work when they leave two dead on the field."

"So do I," answered the major, "and that is why I inquired of old Zook for particulars. He is the last man in the ranks to be exaggerative or sensational, and as for his captain,—well, this despatch is simply characteristic of Terry. He has a horror of anything 'spread-eagle,' as he calls it, and will never praise officers or men; says that it must be considered as a matter of course that they behaved well and did their duty. Otherwise he would be sure to prefer charges. Now, Dr. Bayard, if you will kindly send for Dr. Weeks I will give him his instructions, and, meantime, will you make such preparations as may be necessary?"

This the "Chesterfield of the Medical Department" could not but understand as a hint to be off, and he promptly arose and signified his readiness to carry out any wishes the commanding officer might have. Holmes, too, arose and started for the door with his host and entertainer, and, though the major called him back and asked if he would not remain, he promptly refused, saying that he greatly wished to accompany the doctor and see the preparations made in such cases.

But he tarried only a few moments with Bayard at the hospital, and when the doctor strove to detain him he begged to be excused a little while. There was a matter, he said, he wanted to look into before those ambulances started. The post surgeon gazed after him in some wonderment as the Chicagoan strode away, and tried to conjecture what could be taking him back to the house at this moment. Nellie was not to be seen, and he knew of no other attraction.

But Mr. Holmes had no idea of going to the surgeon's quarters. Over near the block-house he saw Mr. Hatton with his little party returning from their inglorious mission to Sudstown,—the lieutenant disgustedly climbing the slope, while a brace of his assistants, the guards, were chuckling and chatting in a low tone together, evidently extracting more amusement from their recent duty than did the officer of the day. Joining Hatton and allaying his anxiety by telling him the particulars of Captain Terry's despatch,—supplemented by the information that McLean's injuries were not considered serious,—Mr.

Holmes asked permission to send one of the men in quest of Zook, with whom he desired very much to speak.

"He has gone to the stable, sir, to take care of his horse," said a corporal of the guard.

"If you are in a hurry to see him, Mr. Holmes, perhaps the best way would be to go to the troop stables. Yonder they are, down that slope to the north. He must attend to his horse,—groom and care for him before he can leave; and then, I fancy, he will be mighty glad of something to eat. I'll send for him if you wish, and tell him to come as soon as he's through his duties. Where will you have him call,—at the doctor's?"

"No, I believe not. If it is all the same to you, would you mind my seeing him at your quarters? I am greatly interested in this scout and fight, and want to get his story of the affair. Terry doesn't tell anything but the baldest outline."

"Certainly, Mr. Holmes. My room,—that is, McLean's, be it. The door is open, and I'll be out of your way by that time. I'm going at once to ask the adjutant to take my sword, and get the major to let me go down for Mac."

"The ambulance is being put in readiness now. I'll go with you to Major Miller's. What time can I best see the corporal?"

"Right after retreat roll-call, just after sunset, I should say. He would like time to spruce up a bit and get supper."

"Then say nine o'clock. I must not leave my host alone at the dinner-table, and I fear Miss Bayard will not be down."

"Is Miss Bayard ill?" asked Mr. Hatton.

"Hardly that! She was greatly overcome by the shock of hearing this news as it was told her. Some idiot of a servant came rushing in, and said a courier was back from Captain Terry's command and that Mr. McLean was killed."

"And she swooned or fainted?" asked Hatton, with evident interest.

"Very nearly," answered Mr. Holmes, with grave face and eyes that never flinched. "I think she would have fallen down the stairs, had she not been caught in the nick of time."

"That will be something poor Mac will hear with comfort."

"Yes," was the decided answer, after an instant of silence. "Yes. It would comfort me if I were in his place. Nine o'clock then, Mr. Hatton, and at your quarters."

Before dark the ambulances got away, Dr. Weeks and the lieutenant going with them on horseback. Cutting short a post-prandial cigar, Mr. Holmes left the surgeon to sip his coffee in solitude when a glance at his watch showed him that the hour of nine was approaching. Quickly he strode over toward "Bedlam," and sprang up the low flight of steps to the veranda. To his surprise, the hall-door was closed; he turned the knob, but there was no yielding. Looking in through the side-lights, he could see that a lamp was burning on the second floor, but that the hall-lantern below had either been forgotten or its light extinguished. Retracing his steps, he decided to go to the quartermaster and ask if he could have the key, but before he had taken thirty strides up the parade he remembered that Hatton had told him that the hall-door was never locked and rarely closed. This struck him as odd, and he stopped to think it over in connection with what he had just observed. Standing there just beyond the southern end of the big, faded white rookery, invisible himself in the darkness, he looked up at the lights in the rooms occupied by the Forrest family, and wondered how the self-possessed and handsome young lady, now occasionally alluded to as the "Queen of Bedlam," had borne the day. The garrison was unusually still; not a sound of mirth, music, or laughter came from the barracks of the men; not a whisper from the quarters of the officers around the parade. Somewhere, perhaps a mile away, out beyond the rushing Laramie, a dog or a coyote was yelping, but all within the old fort was still as death. Suddenly, from the northern end of the veranda, there came the sound of a latch or lock quickly turned, a light footfall on the creaking wooden floor, the swish and swirl of silken skirts, coming toward him rapidly. He gazed with all his eyes, but could not discern the advancing figure; so, struck by a sudden impulse, he sprang to the veranda, up the southern steps, and almost collided with a woman's form, scurrying past him in the darkness.

"I beg pardon, Miss For——" he began to say; but without a word, with sudden leap the slender shape whisked out of reach of voice or hand and vanished into the southern hall-way.

X.

BEFORE the sounding of tattoo that night, the stage came in from Cheyenne. It had been warned by fleeing ranchmen of the presence of the Sioux at Eagle's Nest, and had turned back to the strong defences at "Phillips's," on the Chug, remaining there in security until the driver had satisfied himself that the coast was clear. No passengers came down with him, but he brought the mail; and, as none had been received for two days, and the wires were still down, the major commanding turned out and tramped to the combined stage-station and post-office the moment he was notified of the arrival. Here, while the letters and papers were being distributed, he was accommodated with a chair in Mrs. Griffin's little parlor, and his own personal mail was handed in to him as rapidly as the swift fingers of the postmistress could sort the various missives. Outside, the stage-driver was surrounded by a little crowd of soldiers, scouts, and teamsters, and held forth with frontier descriptive power on the adventures of the night previous. He could "swar" the Sioux had burned a "Black Hills outfit" not far below Eagle's Nest, for he had come far enough this side of the Chug to see the glare in the skies, and had passed the charred remnants just before sundown this very evening. He had heard along the road that there were anywhere from two to five hundred Indians on the raid; and Miller, listening to the eager talk and comparing the estimate of the ranch-people with the experiences of his own campaigning, readily made up his mind that there were probably four or five score of young warriors in the party,—too many, with their magazine rifles, revolvers, and abundant ammunition, for Terry to successfully "tackle" with his little detachment. The major rejoiced that the captain was sensible enough to discontinue the pursuit at the Niobrara crossing. Beyond that there were numerous ridges, winding ravines, even a shallow cañon or two,—the very places for ambuscade; and it would be an easy matter for a small party of the Sioux to drop back and give the pursuers a bloody welcome. No! Terry had done admirably so long as there was a chance of square fighting, and his subsequent moves, barring the one dash down-stream after a "fooling party" while the main body slipped across the ford, had been dictated by sound judgment. He deplored the crippled and depleted condition of his little command, however. Here was Blunt, one of his best cavalry officers, seriously wounded and in high fever;

i

here was McLean, another admirable young soldier, he knew not how seriously wounded; and, with old Bruce laid up with rheumatism, he had not a company officer for duty at the post. The adjutant and quartermaster, the doctor and his own energetic self were the only ones he could count on for the next twenty-four hours, as belonging to the garrison proper. The infantry battalion that had camped down on the flats so short a time before was already beyond his jurisdiction, in march toward Fetterman up the Platte. It was with great relief, therefore, he read that six troops of the —th Cavalry had reached Cheyenne, and were under orders to march to Laramie as soon as supplied with ammunition and equipments for sharp field-service.

Presently he heard the suave tones of Dr. Bayard accosting Mrs. Griffin with anxious inquiries for his letters, and courteous apologies for intruding upon her during "business hours," but he had been without letters or papers so long now, had just heard of the arrival of the stage, Mr. Holmes was visiting him, and would she kindly put any mail there might be for Mr. Holmes in his box? Mrs. Griffin was quite as susceptible to courteous and high-bred and flattering manners as any of her sex, and to her thinking no man in all the army compared with the post surgeon in elegance of deportment. At his bidding she would willingly have left the distribution of the mail to almost any hands and come forth from behind the glass partition to indulge in a chat with him. She would gladly have invited him to step into the little parlor, but the major was already there poring over his letters, and she could not neglect her official duties in the august presence of the post commander. But Mrs. Griffin was all smiles as she handed out the doctor's partially-completed packet, and then, in a low tone, informed him that Major Miller was in the little parlor behind the office, if he saw fit to wait there, and Dr. Bayard, who could not abide being jostled by his fellow-men or even being seen among what he considered the common herd, eagerly availed himself of her offer. Miller looked up and greeted him with a pleasant nod, and immediately read to him the news of the coming of the cavalry battalion from Cheyenne, then bade him pull up a chair and read his letters by the bright "astral" burning on the centre-table. Outside in the hall and corridor in front of the dusty glass partition the crowd had rapidly increased. Not one in a dozen in the gathering had the faintest expectation of getting a letter, but there was no harm in asking and much mental solace, apparently, in cultivating the appearance of a man of the world or a woman of society who was in the daily habit of receiving and responding to a dozen. And so teamsters, laundresses, scouts, "Indian-bound" Black Hillers, and one or two sauntering soldiers were swarming about the porch and hall-way, and jamming in a compact mass in front of the little window whereat the postmistress behind her vitreous barrier was still at work. It was a good-natured, chaffing, laughing crowd, but still one very independent and self-satisfied, after the manner of the frontier, where every man in a mixed gathering is as good as his neighbor, and every woman is as good as she chooses to hold herself. It had made a passage for the commanding officer and afterward for the post surgeon, but that was before it had attained its present proportions. Now when Mr. Roswell Holmes paused at the outskirts with Corporal Zook by his side, some of the loungers looked around with their hands in their pockets; some of the cowboys who had earned their dollars on his ranch nodded cheerily at sight of their employer; but this was the United States post-office, these were sovereign citizens, and every man or woman of them, except the half-dozen enlisted men whose mail was always taken to barracks, had just as much right there as the capitalist from Chicago,—and knew it. So did Mr. Holmes. He returned the greetings as cheerily as they were given; made no attempt to push through, and probably would have remained contentedly until the crowd dispersed and let him in, had not the notes of the infantry bugle sounding first call for tattoo summoned Zook and the other soldiers to make their way to barracks.

"I'm a thousand times obliged to you, Corporal Zook, for all you've told me, and I assure you I'm as proud of the lieutenant as you are. Now, I may not be here when the troop gets back to-morrow,—I may have to go back to see if all is well at the ranch; but after their ride they'll all be thirsty, and when I'm very thirsty there's nothing I like better than a glass of cool lager. There is plenty of it on ice at the trader's, and,—you do the entertaining for me, will you?" And the corporal found his palm invaded by a fold of crisp greenbacks.

"If it's for the troop, sir, I can't say no," answered Zook, with dancing eyes. Pay-day was some weeks off after all, and he knew how "the fellers" would relish the trader's beer. "Now, if you would like to sit down, why not go around to the other side and away from this crowd? There are empty benches at the stage-office. I must run, sir; so good-night, and many thanks."

The office-window had just been thrown open and the distribution was just begun. It would be some time before his turn would come. Holmes knew perfectly well that, only for the fun of the thing, some of those teamsters and scouts would form a "queue," and, with unimpeachable gravity, march up to the window and inquire if there was anything for Red-Handed Bill, or Rip-Roaring Mike, or the Hon. G. Bullwhacker, of Laramie Plains. He wanted time to think a bit before he returned to the doctor's house, anyhow. He had drawn from Corporal Zook a detailed account of McLean's spirited and soldierly conduct in the fight; learned that it was he who killed the second warrior in what was practically a hand-to-hand struggle, and that his wounds were painful and severe, despite his effort to overcome and hide them when the pursuit began. Hatton's remarks had been echoing time and again through his memory. It would indeed be comfort to McLean to hear how shocked and painfully stricken was Nellie Bayard at the news of the fight and his probable death. If it proved half the comfort to McLean that it was sorrow to his elderly rival, thought Holmes with a deep sigh, "he'll soon be well, and 'twill be high time for me to vanish."

Pacing slowly up the road, he turned an angle of the old wooden building, and found himself alone in a broad, square enclosure. The stars were shining brightly overhead, but there was no moon and the darkness in this nook among the storehouses and offices was simply intense. The only light came through the slats of the shutter at a side-window back of the post-office. Merely glancing at it as he passed,

Holmes walked on with bowed head and hands clasped behind him, thinking deeply over the situation. Had he come too late to win that sweet, youthful, guileless heart, or had he come only just in time to see it given to another? Had he, in the light of what he had seen and heard, any right to speak of matters that had gravely distressed him? Was it his bounden duty to disclose certain suspicions, display certain proofs? Or was it more than all his, the man's, part to stay and help to sweep aside the web that was unquestionably weaving about that brave-faced, clear-eyed, soldierly young subaltern? Despite Bayard's detractions; despite Mrs. Miller's whispered confession that there was a thief in their midst; despite the fact that his wallet was stolen from the overcoat-pocket when no one, to his knowledge, but McLean himself had been there; despite the discovery on the floor—in front of his bureau—of a handkerchief embroidered with McLean's initials; despite the fact that it was known that he had been placed heavily in debt by the stoppage of his pay,—Mr. Roswell Holmes could not find it in his heart to believe that the young soldier could be guilty of theft. He would not believe it of him, even as a rival.

Then there was another thing. Who was the silken-skirted woman he met in the darkness but an hour or so before,—the woman whom he had attempted to accost, but who slipped past him like a will-o'-the-wisp—in silence? How was it that the door to Hatton's hall was closed and locked, when Hatton told him it was always open? Why was it that the light in that lower hall was extinguished, and by whom was it done? Had he not gone thither almost immediately after recovering from the surprise of his encounter on the veranda, and found the hospital attendant grumblingly relighting it? The man had heard some queer, swishing sound, he explained, as he sat by Mr. Blunt's bedside, and "something that sounded like drawers being opened in the room below." He stepped out in the hall, he said, just in time to hear the lock of the front door hastily turned, and somebody go stealthily and quickly out on the veranda, "swishing" all the way. The ladies had been over along the upper gallery two or three times, to bring cool drinks to Mr. Blunt's door and inquire how he was getting on,—Mrs. Post and the young lady, Miss Forrest, he meant,—but they wouldn't want anything in Mr. McLean's rooms down-stairs. The man looked curiously up at Mr. Holmes as he told his tale. Holmes was puzzled too, but bade him keep quiet. Some one of the servants, perhaps, who wanted a match, he suggested; but the little soldier shook his head. Servants didn't wear dresses that "swished" like that.

The crowd was beginning to thin considerably, as Holmes could tell by the sound of receding voices. He decided that it was about time for him to move and get his own mail, when he became aware of something dark and shapeless crouching along close under the post-office end of the building and slowly and cautiously approaching the window from which the light was streaming. At first he thought it some big dog scratching his side along the cleats of the wooden wall, but as he stood silently observing the dim shadow it was evident that no quadruped was thus warily creeping toward him. Holmes stood leaning against a storehouse platform in the deepest shade of an overhanging roof; the figure was perhaps twelve or thirteen yards away, and, as it neared the window, the vague outlines of the mysterious creature became more easily discernible. Immediately under the beams of light that shot across the dark enclosure the figure paused; slowly raised itself; a hand went up to the head and whipped off a cap just as the crown was tinged by the gleam from within. Holmes distinctly saw the reflection of the light on the brightly polished brass of the device, but could not make out whether the device itself was the crossed rifles of the infantry or sabres of the cavalry. Then the hand was laid upon the sill, the body slowly unbent, and the head was raised until two beady eyes, under a low fore cad and a crop of thick, dark hair, could peer in between the slats. One lingering scrutiny of every person and object visible in the room, then down he crouched, and, almost on all-fours, slipped away to the corner of the building, Holmes now briskly striding in pursuit. Half-way back across the court, just as he entered the beam of light, the latter's foot came down upon the edge of one of those tough and elastic hoops, such as are sure to be lying about in the yards of commissary and quartermaster storehouses, and in the twinkling of an eye it whirled up and struck him with a sharp and audible snap. In an instant the crouching figure shot to its full height and darted out of sight around the corner. When Holmes reached the front of the building, not a man in uniform was visible. Cowboys and a scout or two remained. The stage-driver was again the centre of attraction, and all were grouped about him on the low piazza. Holmes called one of the ranchmen to one side, and asked him if he had seen or heard anything of a soldier who came suddenly around the corner, but the man shook his head. Stepping inside the office he met the major and his host, Dr. Bayard, while a tall, well-formed, colored girl stood in front of the little wicket, and a number of loungers still hung about the place. The officers stopped and said they would wait until he got his letters, and, as he took his place near the window,

Mrs. Griffin was just handing a little packet to the colored girl. The light fell on the topmost letter, addressed in bold, legible hand to Miss Fanny Forrest; and Holmes could plainly see the post-mark and device on the upper corner, showing that it came from the Red Cloud Agency, and old Camp Robinson. "Halloo!" thought he to himself, "I had forgotten that we were as good as cut off from them now, and they are sending around by way of Sidney and Cheyenne." Quickly the girl turned over the letters, made some laughing remark expressive of disappointment at getting nothing from her beau; then, facing Mr. Holmes and showing her white teeth, with a coquettish toss of her head accosted him: "Good-evening, Mr. Holmes. S'pose you don't know me; I'm Celestine,—Miss Forrest's girl. Miss Griffin, yere's Mr. Holmes waitin' for his mail. Ain't no use you lookin' for anything for this trash," she said, contemptuously indicating the two or three intervening frontier folks. "Han' it to me an' I'll give it to him."

But just at this moment there was a stir at the door. The loungers who had never budged an inch for Mr. Holmes drew promptly back, making way for a tall young lady, who entered, all aglow from a rapid walk, her dark eyes gleaming, her fine, mobile lips wreathed with pleasant smiles the instant she caught sight of the doctor, who, cap in hand, advanced to meet her. It was Miss Forrest herself, and behind her came her escort, the adjutant.

"I thought I heard Celestine's voice," she said, looking questioningly around; and Holmes quickly noted that the girl had suddenly slunk back behind a little group of camp-women. Finding it useless to evade the searching glance of her young mistress, the girl came forth.

"Yes, Miss Fanny. I got your letters, miss," she said, but the confident tone was gone. Holmes marked the look in Miss Forrest's flashing eye as she took the little packet with no gentle hand. He was near enough, too, to hear the low-spoken but clearly enunciated words:

"And I told you néver again to touch my letters. This must be the last time."

XI.

FOUR days had passed since Terry's fight down the river. McLean, painfully wounded, but very quiet and plucky, had been re-established in his old quarters at "Bedlam." Dr. Bayard, after one or two somewhat formal visits, had relinquished the entire charge of the case to his assistant; so that Dr. Weeks was now the medical and surgical attendant of both the young officers in the north hall, while his senior continued assiduously to care for the wants of the feminine colony in the other. It may be said right here, that, so far as those sturdy "refugees" the Posts were concerned, professional and personal attentions from Dr. Bayard were both declared unnecessary. Mrs. Post was a woman of admirable physique and somewhat formidable personality. She did not fancy the elaborate manners of the surgeon at their first meeting, and allowed her lack of appreciation of "His Elegancy" to develop into positive dislike before she had known him a fortnight. Now, since the "north end" had become a hospital, she was willing to admit the doctor to her confidence, for the good lady was incessant in the preparation of comforting drinks or culinary dainties for the two invalids; but what was the measure of her indignation when she discovered that Bayard's attentions at "Bedlam" were confined to the south hall and to Mrs. Forrest's quarters?

He had always been a specialist in the maladies of women and children, to be sure, and we all know of what vital importance are such practitioners in our large garrisons. He was a welcome visitor either at the fireside or in the sick-room of every family homestead on the reservation—except Mrs. Post's—whensoever he chose to call, but that his presence at Mrs. Forrest's should be requisite and necessary three or four times every twenty-four hours was something Mrs. Post could not be brought to believe, and her scepticism speedily inoculated the entire community.

Mrs. Forrest declared she did not know how she could have lived through the terrors of the past week had it not been for Dr. Bayard's delicate and skilful ministrations. The doctor himself was understood to say that the poor lady's nervous system was utterly unstrung, that she was in a hyper-sensitive condition which might readily develop into nervous prostration unless she was carefully guarded. The officers of the garrison, when they spoke of the matter at all, which was not often, laughingly referred to the admirable tactics of the astute physician in finding excuses for frequent professional visits to a house where it was now apparent to all he was personally interested. The women, when they did not speak of the matter to one another, which was seldom indeed, were divided in their opinions. That Dr. Bayard was "smitten" with Fanny Forrest was something they had seen from the start, but that brilliant and most incomprehensible young woman had on more than one occasion treated him with marked coldness and aversion. What was the matter? Had he been too precipitate in his wooing? Twice since Hatton returned with his little escort, bringing in the wounded, had Miss Forrest declined Dr. Bayard's arm, and, on the other hand, while she seemed to repel the senior, she was now showing a marked interest in his junior,—the attendant of the wounded officers. Twice while Dr. Bayard was known to be visiting at the Forrests', she was seen to come forth, and, after an irresolute glance up and down the walk, as though she had no other purpose in venturing out than to escape from her elderly admirer, the young lady had walked down the path away from the officers' quarters and disappeared from view in the direction of the trader's store. Some of the ladies were beginning to believe that, *faute de mieux*, the doctor was consoling himself in a flirtation with his lackadaisical patient; but it was speedily noted that he stayed only a few moments when Miss Forrest left the premises, and the idea was as speedily scouted by the entire sisterhood, unless, indeed, we except the lady herself. Poor Mrs. Forrest! In these days of her faded beauty, she could not forget the fact that it was only a. few years before that her rosebud complexion and tender blue eyes had been the cause of many a heartache among the young fellows in the garrison where she, the only damsel, reigned supreme; and lives there a woman who, having once queened it over the hearts of the opposite sex, can quite abandon the idea that her powers still exist?

Knowing, from plain declarations to that effect, that her spirited sister-in-law totally disapproved of Dr. Bayard after a conversation held with him the night McLean was returned to the post, Mrs. Forrest was fain to flatter herself that these frequent visits to her were impelled by an interest transcending the professional and rapidly becoming sentimental.. It really did her good; gave her something to think about besides her woes; rescued her from the slatternly ways into which she was falling and restored a faded coquetry to her dress and mien; brightened her dreary eyes and lent color to her pallid cheek, and prompted her to surround herself with those domestic barricades against unhallowed glances and unwarranted sighs,— the children. But when Fanny Forrest flatly told her it was all nonsense, this encouraging Dr. Bayard's visits on account of some supposititious malady, and that she was looking better than she had seen her look in six months, the lady took offence at the first statement and alarm at the second, and between the two a relapse was accomplished which, of course, triumphantly established the justice of her position and the ineffable cruelty of her sister's charge.

Fanny Forrest's life could hardly have been pleasant just then, said superficial commentators. To every woman who called upon the lady of the house in her invalid state, Mrs. Forrest had something to say about the heartlessness and utter lack of sympathy with which she was treated; and who can doubt that the letters she wrote her soldier husband made frequent complaint to the same effect? Now, if in the domestic circle Miss Forrest had no friend or sympathizer, it was quite as bad without. With all her frankness, brilliancy, and dash, with all her willingness to be cordial and friendly, there had arisen between her and the whole sisterhood in the garrison a strange, intangible, but impenetrable barrier. She was welcome nowhere, and was too proud to inquire the cause.

This state of things could not go on long, as a matter of course. Sooner or later the reason would be demanded by somebody, and then the stories would come out. Mrs. Miller and Mrs. Bruce, as recorded in an earlier chapter, had covenanted together to keep the secret; but that mysterious theft the night of the dinner at the doctor's had made the former determine on another revelation to her lord and master, the post commander. As for Mrs. Bruce, she struggled—well, womanfully—to hold her tongue, and womanfully succeeded.

Two nights after McLean had been brought home and was lying in a somewhat feverish condition, the major commanding came in and softly tapped at the door of the front room. Hatton was seated at the table reading by the light of the Argand, and he arose at once and tiptoed to see who was there.

"Oh! Come in, major," he said, in a low tone, throwing open the door. "Come in."

"Is McLean asleep?" whispered the major. "I—I don't want to disturb him. I only wanted to inquire."

"Not asleep, sir, but lying in a sort of doze. Weeks is trying to fight off fever."

"I know; I understand. It may be several days before he'll be well enough to—to talk, won't it?" and the major gazed keenly into Hatton's eyes, and Hatton plainly saw the trouble in his commander's face.

"I fear it may, sir. Weeks says he must be kept quiet and free from worry of any kind."

The major paused, irresolute. He took off his forage-cap and mopped his brow with his handkerchief, then stood there twisting the cap in his hands. He looked down the dim hall-way, then through the crack of the door, then down at his boots, and all the time Hatton stood there holding wide open the door, yet hoping and praying he would not come in. Something told the lieutenant that the matter so plainly worrying the commanding officer was one neither he nor McLean could speak of if it could possibly be helped.

But Miller was in sore trouble, and he could not stand alone.

"Hatton!" he muttered, impulsively, "is the nurse there? Can you come out with me? I—I have heard something that gives me a world of concern, something I must ask you about. I can't talk of it here. Sick men's ears are sometimes far more acute than those of their sound and healthy brothers. Can you come now?"

"I am alone with Mac just now, sir. I sent the attendant down to the post-office and the store. He had been cooped up all day, and was grateful for a litttle fresh air. When he returns——" and Hatton stopped vaguely. He knew it might be an hour before the man got back. That would give him time to think.

"Well. That will have to do. Come to my quarters then, and, if a lot of women are there, you

—you say you want to see me about something,—anything,—and I'll come out. I don't want them to dream I'm investigating anything." And here the major stopped uneasily and glanced up-stairs; then looked inquiringly at Hatton. "Who's up there?" he asked.

"No one, sir, to my knowledge. Blunt's door is closed and he is sleeping. Weeks was there not ten minutes since, and stopped to see me on the way down. Why do you ask?"

"Why, I thought I heard something,—a woman's dress and light footfall. I even thought I saw a shadow at the head of the stairs."

Hatton's heart gave a great thump, and he felt his face glowing under his commander's gaze, but he answered steadily.

"It is possible, sir. Mrs. Post and Miss Forrest both have been coming along the upper gallery frequently, bringing things to both Blunt and McLean. Mrs. Post comes over to inquire every hour or so, and they tiptoe in and out as light as a kitten. Shall I run up and see?"

"Oh, no,—no! If that's the explanation, it is simple enough. No, I'm all upset. I—I fancied there was some one listening. Come to me as soon as you can, Hatton. By the way, have you heard from Mr. Holmes?"

"No, sir. He was called suddenly to the ranch, and I presume he is there."

"I know, I know. But did he see McLean before he left?"

"See him! Yes, sir; but that's about all he could do. McLean was in no condition to receive visitors, and Weeks hustled him out somewhat unceremoniously."

"Well. That's all, just now. I'll expect you soon after tattoo."

"Very good, sir."

And then the major went away, closing the hall-door after him. Hatton stood there a moment as though rooted to the spot, his brow moistening with beads of sweat that seemed starting from every pore. Despite his secrecy, then, despite McLean's destruction of the evidence of her visit the night of the disappearance of their property, despite their determination to shield the sister of an absent comrade from suspicion, or disgrace, in some way the story must have gotten around. Possibly there were other thefts of which he knew nothing, in which suspicion had pointed to her. Possibly the vague confessions, implicating no one, which he had made to Mrs. Miller, taken in connection with events of which he had no knowledge, had proved sufficient to weave a chain of circumstantial evidence about her; and now the commanding officer was aroused, and was coming down on him, and poor Mac yonder, for full details of their losses and their knowledge of the affair. He would give anything to secure the postponement of that dreaded interview until he could talk over matters with his comrade, but when would that be a possibility? Just as soon as the attendant returned, he must go to his commander, and either make a clean breast of it or refuse to utter a word. What course would he ask or expect of a comrade if it were his, Hatton's, sister, who was here alone and defenceless? By heaven, McLean was right! They must shield her, so far as shield of theirs could serve, until Forrest himself could come to be her adviser and protector.

Then he, too, stopped, listened, and looked up the stairs. Then he, too, started, but with a start to which the major's sudden turn was a mere languid gesture. Hardly could he believe his eyes; hardly could he trust his reeling senses, but it was she,— Fanny Forrest,—not standing at the head of the stairs, but coming swiftly down upon him, her finger at her lips, her other hand gathering her skirts so that they should make as little rustle as possible as she swooped quickly down the stairs. Another instant, and she was at his side, her eyes gleaming like fiery coals, her face burning, her lips firm, set, and determined. He was too much startled to speak. It was she who broke the silence, in words clear-cut and distinct yet soft and low.

"Mr. Hatton, I saw your major coming here. I have heard within two days more than you know. I know why he wishes to see you to-night, and—yes, I listened. There is more at stake than you dream of. Now, I hasten to you; there is no time to explain,—no time to answer questions. If you would save a friend from wrong or ruin, don't go near Major Miller to-night. I adjure you, find some excuse. I'll find one for you, if it is only to delay that attendant; but mark what I say, don't go near Major Miller to-night, or tell him what you know until Mr. Holmes returns. I—I've sent for him. Will you promise?"

"Promise!" he utters, slowly, a dazed look in his eyes. "Good God, Miss Forrest! I would do anything in my power for Captain Forrest's sister, and for him; but if—if this thing is known, what can my silence avail?"

"Never mind Captain Forrest or Captain Forrest's sister! This is vital! Do you promise? It is only for a day. Mr. Holmes will be here in twenty-four hours."

"What can his coming or going—pardon me! but

I'm at a loss to see how he is in any way concerned."

A manly step was heard on the porch without. She turned a glance of terror at the hall-door and flew to spring the latch, but the step went on toward the south hall.

"It is the doctor," she said, falteringly. "He is going to our quarters, and I must hurry back the way I came. Mr. Hatton, tell no one I came to you here; and, as for the rest, I implore you to be guided by what I say. One thing more,"—she whipped from her pocket a white silk handkerchief. "Put this back among his,—not on top, but anywhere among them otherwise."

And, thrusting the soft fabric into his hand, without another word she flew up the old wooden stairs, her skirts rushing and "swishing" over the floor, her slippered feet twinkling over the rickety flight, light as kittens, swift as terriers; and in an instant she was through the upper hall, out on the gallery, and beyond sight and hearing. A few moments, dazed and confounded, Hatton stood there gazing vacantly after her. Then he thought he heard McLean's voice, and entering found him propped on his elbow, a queer look on his face.

"Hat, there are spooks in this old rookery. I could have sworn I heard a woman's dress and a woman's footfalls on those creaking stairs just now. Has any one been in here?"

"N—no one, Mac."

"Gad! I'm not dreaming. It sounded just as it did the night—the night that thing happened. You know, Hat."

XII.

JUST at tattoo that evening Mrs. Miller was smitten with a sudden desire to go over and see Nellie Bayard. The child hadn't been out of the house, she explained, since "the Grays" started for the fray down the Platte, taking Randall McLean with them. She longed to see her and learn from her lips how matters were going at home. She wondered if Nellie knew how her father was devoting himself to the Forrests; she wondered if the gentle and obedient daughter would not rebel at the idea of such a possibility as his becoming seriously attached to Miss Forrest. She had indulged the major in one very plain and startling dissertation on the subject of that young woman, from the effects of which he was still suffering; but, worst of all, her motherly heart longed to acquire, through Nellie's words, looks, or actions, some idea as to whether she really cared for her pet among all the lieutenants. Of course Nellie liked — but did she love him? Of McLean's deep-rooted regard for the shy and sensitive little maiden, Mrs. Miller had not the shadow of a doubt. Nellie had no one, she argued, to be a mother to her in this troublesome time, and yet she was beginning to feel a species of jealousy in the knowledge that the Bruces and the Gordons and other good garrison people—maid and matron—had been seen going continually to and from the doctor's quarters. Mrs. Miller thought she had a prior claim on the confidences of the doctor's pretty daughter, and did not relish it that others should possibly be before her. Oddly enough there was no one calling on this night of nights; the major had been out, ostensibly to attend to business at the office, but something told her he was seeking information as to the array of circumstances pointing to the fact that there was further evidence against Miss Forrest. . The bugles were sounding the call through the stillness of the early summer night, though at Laramie summer seemed yet far away, when she heard him coming heavily up the steps to the piazza. Well the good lady knew by the very cadence of his footfalls just what mood possessed him. It was slow, draggy, spiritless to-night; and, though he had almost angrily and contemptuously checked her when she began the story of these later revelations, her heart yearned over him now. She went down to him, as he sat there looking drearily out at the twinkling lights across the parade.

"Come, major," she said, addressing him, as was a fancy of hers at times, by the formal army title instead of the Christian name. "Come; I'm going over to the doctor's to see how Nellie is to-night; and, not that I need an escort, I want your company. A glass of his old Madeira will do you good, and he is always so glad to offer it. You are blue to-night, and so am I. Come."

He resisted faintly. Hatton might be along any moment, and he had an appointment with him, he said; but she speedily settled that by calling the orderly, and telling him, should Mr. Hatton call, to come over at once to Dr. Bayard's and let the major know. Then her obedient lord had no further objections to urge, and he, too, had bethought him of the doctor's Madeira and those incomparable Regalia Britannicas. Nowhere in Wyoming were there cigars to match Bayard's, and it was easy to persuade himself that he could so much better deliberate on the matter in hand over the fragrance of the soothing Havana. Robert threw open the door in hospitable Virginian style at sight of the commandant and his wife, ushered them into the parlor, sent the maid up-stairs to inquire if Miss Elinor could see Mrs. Miller; and then, true to his Southern training, reappeared in the parlor with a decanter of wine and some flaky "Angels' food" upon a silver salver. The doctor had gone to the hospital, he explained, but would soon return. Then he vanished. Miller smacked his lips over the

Madeira, and smilingly admitted to his better half that he believed there were some things on which "her head was leveller than his."

For a reply she pointed to the hall-way.

"Come here just one moment. I want you to see where I stood, and how I could view what was going on at the hat-rack out there."

Silently he stood by her side, glanced at the mirror, and noted the reflection therein.

"It was just there his beautiful fur coat was hanging,—and the money in its pocket," she said.

Then came the message from aloft, that, if Mrs. Miller would step up-stairs, Miss Bayard would be glad to see her,—Miss Bruce was already there; and so the major was left alone. He sat some five minutes looking over an album or two, poured out and drank another glass of wine, and bethought him that Bayard had told him if ever he felt like smoking to go right into his study and help himself. Now was the very time. A dozen strides brought him to the broad-topped library-table littered with books, pamphlets, papers of all kinds, and among them the inviting-looking brown box. Another moment, and, ensconced in the big easy-chair, with a fragrant Regalia between his lips and a late New York paper in his hand, the major was forgetting the perplexities of the day. The reading-lamp he found lighted threw a bright glow upon the paper in his hand, but left the apartment in darkness. Out in the kitchen he could faintly hear the voices of the domestics and the sound of crockery and glass in process of cleaning, above-stairs the murmur of softer tongues. All in the front part of the house on the first floor was silent. Presently, out on the parade the bugler began to sound the signal, "taps," to extinguish lights, and at the same moment Miller heard the click of the latch at the front door. There had been no footsteps that he could hear, and he thought he might be mistaken. He listened intently, and presently click, click, it went again. Odd, thought Miller. That is not the way a man enters his own house, nor does it sound like the way an honest man enters any one else's. Click, click, again, louder and more forcibly now. Some one was plainly trying to open that door without attracting the attention of the occupants. What if now he should be able to surprise the prowler? What if this should, indeed, prove to be some one bent on larceny or worse? Now was an excellent time. The doctor was known to be away,—over at the hospital. Miss Bayard was known to be up-stairs, confined to her room. Very probably the thief had watched the movements of the post surgeon, knew he would be detained some time, and—there were all those pretty nicknacks in the parlor. There was that handsome silver in the dining-room (it was always in the doctor's strong box under the bed at night). What more likely than that now was the time selected by some sharp sneak-thief in the garrison to slink through the shadows of the night to the doctor's quarters, slip in the front way while the servants were all chattering and laughing in the kitchen in the rear, and make off with his plunder? It was an inspiration. Miller's heart fairly bounded at the thought. If the thief could enter now, he could have entered before,—the night of the dinner. By Jove! Did he not recall that sudden gust of cold air that swept from the hall in the midst of the doctor's story? Click, click, snap! At it again, and no mistake this time. Quickly and on tiptoe the major stole toward the hall where he could see the front door. It was his hope, his belief now, that the thief would speedily effect an entrance; and from the darkness of his lair the major could see and identify him, let him in, follow him on tiptoe to the dining-room, there seize and confound him in the very act, and so, fastening the crime on some one guilty man, dispel at once and for all the cloud of suspicion that hovered over a woman's fair fame. Click, click, again. What was the matter? Would the stubborn lock not yield? or was this a 'prentice hand, and his tools unsuited to the job? In his wild impatience he could have rushed to the door and hurled it open, but that would have only spoiled the game. He could have caught his prowler, but proved nothing. No, patience! patience! A burst of jolly Ethiopian laughter from the distant kitchen drowned for a moment other sounds and possibly unnerved the operator at the door. Did he hear quick, light footsteps hurrying away? There was a broad "stoop" there, quite a wide veranda in fact, since the unsightly wooden storm-door had been removed. For an instant he certainly thought he heard scurrying footfalls. Not the steps themselves, but the creak of the dry woodwork underneath them. He listened intently another moment, but the attempt had apparently been abandoned.

Then—there it was again. Surely he heard a light footfall on the steps,—on the piazza itself. He could bear the suspense no longer, and, springing into the hall where the hanging lamp shed its broad glare over every object, hurled open the door,—and recoiled in mingling agony and horror. God of heaven! There stood Fanny Forrest!

"Major Miller!" she gasped, affrighted at his vehemence and the ghastly look with which he greeted her. "How—how you startled me! Why, what has happened? where were you going in such—why, major—what is the matter?" and now there was something imperious in the demand.

For all answer he could only pass his hand over his quivering face in a dazed, dumb sort of way a moment. Then, rallying suddenly, he stepped forward, giving his head a shake and striving to be cool and calm.

"You are more startled than I, Miss Forrest. I never thought to find you at that door."

"And why not me? I have not seen Nellie since her illness, and came over at taps to inquire if she would not receive me a moment."

"Why—why didn't you ring?" he hoarsely asked.

"Ring! What opportunity had I? My foot had hardly touched the piazza before the door opened in my face and revealed you looking—well, pardon me, Major Miller—as if you had suddenly encountered a ghost."

"Do you mean you have only just come?" he asked.

"Certainly."

"And you saw no one? There was no one here as you came in the gate?"

"Not a soul,—stop a minute though,—there was something——"

"Pray, what are you talking about, Major Miller, and to whom are you talking?" queried the voice of his better half at this very instant; and before he could respond there came through the gate-way and up the steps the debonair, portly doctor.

l   14*

"What!" exclaimed Bayard. "Miss Forrest! Ah, you truant, we've been wondering where you were, your sister and I. Ah, major!—Mrs. Miller. Why, this is delightful! Now indeed am I welcome home! Come right into my parlor, said the—but I'm no spider. Come, Miss Forrest, I know you want to see my little girl,—I left Jeannie Bruce with her. Major, you and I want a glass of Madeira and Mrs. Miller to bless the occasion, and then we all want some music, don't we? Come in, and welcome."

And so, half urging, half pushing, half leading, the doctor swept his trio of visitors into the parlor. Despite her start at Miller's appearance at the door, despite his preoccupation and gloom, which several glasses of the doctor's good wine failed to dissipate, Miss Forrest remained after a brief visit to the invalid up-stairs and, saying that she had promised Nellie, sang to them witchingly again and again.

But that night, despatches flashed in from Fetterman that gave the major another turn. The telegraph operator himself came running up with the message just as the party at the doctor's (considerably augumented by this time by new-comers drawn thither by Miss Forrest's voice) was breaking up for the night. Indians had appeared in great numbers along the North Platte, threatening the road connecting the two posts, and a train had been attacked and burned midway between them. Terry and his hard-worked Grays were ready in an hour to take the trail, but there were no young gallants to ride forth this time. Hatton, indeed, offered his services, but was told he could not be spared. Morning brought tidings that the war-parties were seen only seven miles away at sunrise; and in the presence of the common foe the major, for the time being, put aside the matter weighing so heavily on his mind, but not for a moment could he forget her startled face as he threw open that door. It was time indeed to look the situation squarely through and through. It might be necessary to send for Forrest.

Another day brought with it a strong column of cavalry hastening up from the railway at Cheyenne, and these troops were to be fully provided with rations and ammunition before setting forth toward the Black Hills, whither they were ordered. It was bustle and business for everybody. The major said no more to Hatton on the subject of the interrupted interview; but on the second day, as McLean was lying languidly in his bed, listening to the sounds of hoofs and heels without, and bemoaning his fate that he was to be bedridden here when such stirring times were ahead, his soldier servant came noiselessly to ask the lieutenant's permission to step out a little while to see some friends in the cavalry. The at-

.tendant was seated in the front room, so the permission was readily granted.

"Is there anything the lieutenant wants, sir, before I go?"

"Nothing except a handkerchief. Give me one of those silk ones in this corner of the drawer. They are softer."

The man handed the topmost of the pile, and went noiselessly away. McLean shook it open, and a card dropped out upon the coverlet. Surprised, he picked it up and slowly read it, perplexity and then symptoms of annoyance showing plainly in his face. Twice — thrice he read it through. Then, stowing it under his pillow, he began to think.

Dr. Weeks came in before a great while to renew the dressing on his wound, and asked him if he had not been talking too much.

"I haven't been talking at all. Why do you ask?"

"Pulse a little quicker than it was. What have you been doing?"

"Nothing—to speak of. What is there to do but read and think?"

"You mustn't get to fretting because you can't go out with every expedition, Mac. We all know you'd like it, but you can't have your pie and eat it. You can't get shot in one fight and expect to get into the next. If you'll keep quiet here, I think I can put you in saddle again in a month,—much quicker than I can poor Blunt; but you must be patient, especially now that you'll miss Hatton. He goes out with the train-guard to-night."

"Hatton! To-night?" exclaimed the invalid.

"There you go again, Mac! What a bundle of tow you are, to be sure; I might just as soon touch a match to a magazine."

"Doctor, tell Hatton I want him,—must see him before he goes."

"Confound it, man, I told him to keep away. Why do you want him?"

"*Because I must* see him. You'll have a crazy man on your hands if you don't." And Weeks decided it best to let this headstrong Highlander have his way.

That night, in his field-dress and all ready to start, Hatton gently came to his comrade's bedside.

"What is it, old man?" he asked. "Weeks told me first to slip away without saying good-by,—I'll only be gone a week,—and then hunted me up and said you wanted to see me."

McLean looked out in the front room.

"Send that man away for a while," he said.

"Now for it," groaned Hatton, between his teeth.

"Something new, and he's got hold of it. How in heaven am I to keep my story to myself?"

Obediently at a word from Hatton, the hospital attendant took his cap and stepped outside. Then McLean put forth his hand and took that of the senior lieutenant.

"Hat, you and I have been good friends, haven't we?"

"Always, Mac."

"I've something to ask you. Something I must know. You remember the night we burned that handkerchief?"

"I should say so."

"Have you ever seen—have you ever known of her ever being in here—or around here since?"

Hatton hesitated.

"Tell me, Hat."

"I can't tell you, Mac. There's been the devil to pay. Some other things stolen. Miller's got hold of it, and, old man, I'm thankful I'm going, for I'd have to tell what we know."

"Great God! and Forrest two weeks' march away, —least count! See here, Hat! To-day I found something among my handkerchiefs—in a missing one that was returned. Do you know how it got there?"

"Yes," slowly. "She herself gave it to me and asked me to put it there."

"You don't mean it! How could she, without exciting more suspicion? She must have known it would only make you connect her with what had happened here."

"Mac,—old man; it's no use! I can't keep it back from you. Why! She was reckless of anything I might think. It has gone far beyond suspicion. It is certainty. She was on the watch the night Miller came here for me. It was her dress— her steps you heard in the hall. It may be kleptomania,—God knows; but whatever it is, she threw off all disguise. She listened to Miller's orders that I should come to him at tattoo; and then, the moment he was gone, down she flew to where I stood there at the door, and implored me, Mac, as I would save her from disgrace and ruin not to go— not to tell him."

"And she was not out of her mind?"

"She is as sane as you or I, Mac, except on that one thing."

XIII.

For several days after Hatton's sudden departure Lieutenant McLean was worse. High fever had set in, and Dr. Weeks hardly knew how to account for it. Mrs. Miller, kind soul, had begged to be allowed to come over and help nurse him, and was more than perplexed when, having easily obtained the approval of the post surgeon, she was met by a most embarrassed but earnest negative on the part of his assistant. As Weeks was in charge of the case, Dr. Bayard's sense of professional etiquette would not permit of his opposing his junior in the matter, but did not prevent his expressing himself as surprised and annoyed at what he termed a slight to the wife of the commanding officer. The lady herself could not refrain from telling her husband and making some trenchant criticisms at the expense of the younger physician; and, as a result of her remarks, Old Miller decided to do a thing to which, hitherto, he had always declared himself averse,—namely, to require of his surgical staff a defence of their policy in the matter. He would not do this formally or officially, but he meant to ask Dr. Bayard at once what possible objection there could be to Mrs. Miller's looking in on the young officer and doing what she could to promote his comfort. She was welcome to go to Blunt's bedside, she told him, and Mr. Blunt's wounds were of a more severe character than those of the young infantryman, whom she was virtually forbidden to see.

Miller's honest heart was filled full of perplexities and cares at this time, and the best of men are apt to be a trifle irritable under such conditions. His brow was moody and his step more energetic than usual, as he sallied forth in search of his senior surgeon, this bright sunshiny morning. No one was on the Bayards' piazza, but the front door was open, and, hearing subdued voices in the parlor, he ventured to step inside and tap at the inner door which also stood ajar. It was at once thrown wide open by Janet Bruce, whose bonnie face lighted up with pleasure at sight of him; she had always been a favorite of his from the days when she was a romping maid in short dresses.

"Why, Major Miller! Come right in. Nellie will be so glad to see you."

"What! Is Nellie here?" he asked, and stepping into the parlor, the gloom vanishing from his face at sight of those smiling eyes, he marched over to the sofa where Elinor lay, holding forth to him a white and fragile hand.

"Why, bless your heart, little lady! I'm rejoiced to see you down-stairs again," he cheerily said. "We've all been in the dumps ever since you were taken ill and remanded to bed. And now I suppose you and Janet here have been condoling with each other. With McLean invalided and Hatton on the war-path, I fear me you two young women have been indulging in tears. Hah! Blushing? Well, well, I only wish I were Mac or Hatton either. Enviable fellows, both of them, to have two such pretty girls in mourning for their mishaps. But all the same, don't you lose your hearts to those boys; neither of 'em is worth it." And the major chuckled at the idea of being quizzical and arch.

"Indeed, Major Miller," retorted Miss Bruce, with reddening cheeks and spirited mien. "We're not in mourning at all, though I'm not a whit ashamed of my anxiety about our friends; but as for calling them boys, Mr. Hatton is ten years older than you were when you were married,—Mrs. Miller told me so,—and Mr. McLean has been too many years in the service to be spoken of disparagingly. Have you heard how he is this morning?" she asked, with a sudden change from rebuke to anxious inquiry, flashing a quick glance at his half-averted face as she questioned.

"Not for two hours. I had hoped to find Dr.

Bayard here. Do you know where he is, Miss Nellie?"

"He said he was going to the hospital, major," was the hesitant reply, "but I think he stopped at Bedlam, —at Mrs. Forrest's, perhaps."

"Ah—yes, I remember. Mrs. Forrest does not get well rapidly. Has Miss Forrest been over to see you since you came down-stairs?"

"She called, but papa had desired me to keep very quiet. Janet was reading to me, and she went to the door and saw her."

The major decided to press the question no further. Something in the manner of both girls told him the subject was hardly congenial. He remained a few moments chatting with them, and noted with paternal solicitude the languor and lack of interest in Nellie Bayard's drooping eyes and the unmistakable signs of anxiety and trouble in her sweet face. "My wife is right," he muttered to himself; "she always is, in such things at least,"—for with masculine perversity he could not vouchsafe a sweeping verdict as to a woman's infallibility. "There is small chance here for Holmes," he mentally added. "I only wish young McLean were out of his troubles." And the doctor's hearty voice was heard without, and the tread of feet, and the next moment Bayard was in the hall-way eagerly welcoming a visitor. Miller saw the glance that passed between the girls and the instant cloud of distress that overspread Nellie's face. It was Roswell Holmes again.

"Why! When did you get back?" exclaimed the major, rising. "We had no idea of this. I supposed you would go direct to Cheyenne from the ranch."

"It was my intention, major," answered Mr. Holmes, with grave courtesy, "but letters I received made it preferable that I should come back here, and the doctor kindly gives me an abiding-place. Excuse me," and he passed the major by and went on and bent over the sofa and took Miss Bayard's hand and greeted her with tender intonation in every word, even while he bowed pleasantly to Miss Bruce.

"Quite a surprise, wasn't it?" asked Dr. Bayard from the door-way. "Major, I'm glad to see you here this morning, and no doubt Nellie welcomed you, though she isn't able to play the hostess just yet. We'll have her up and about in a day or two, though. Holmes, old fellow, you can safely hang your traps in the hall now. I've had that latch tinkered up since the night—the night of the dinner. Whoever opened it that night will get fooled on it the next time he tries. I had quite a row with Robert about it, and the conceit was taken out of him not a little."

"Why, how was this, doctor?" asked Miller, with immediate interest. "I had not heard. Are there —have there been any new developments?" And lowering his voice as he asked, the major drew the post surgeon into the hall-way.

"Nothing of consequence, major. Of course we all felt uncomfortable when it was known that Holmes had lost a porte-monnaie from his overcoat-pocket as it hung here on the rack that night. Though he protests there was nothing in it, the thing might have been serious. You remember you thought the hall-door had been opened during our dinner. I believe I was telling some story or other at the time, —bad habit of mine,—and we sent Robert out to look. He came back and said it was tight shut, and couldn't have been open, because he had fixed it so that the latch could not be turned from outside. But Holmes showed us next day that it could be."

"Then you think it had been tampered with,— that some garrison sneak-thief had got in?"

"Well, that's what Holmes says and what Robert stoutly maintains, though you can't see a scratch or a mark or anything to indicate that such means had been used. No, major," and the doctor shook his head ominously. "I—I have another theory, but it's one too shadowy, too unsubstantial to speak of. It is nothing but suspicion."

And Miller would not ask him what it was. Well knowing how the doctor had been devoting himself to Miss Forrest, it was with nothing short of amaze that the old soldier now heard him speak. After all his wife had told him, whom could Bayard mean but the Queen of Bedlam?

Abruptly the major changed the subject, even while thinking how in his own experience he had had recent opportunity to realize the truth of what the doctor said. Somebody had indeed "got fooled on that latch" the night he sat there in the dim light of the doctor's library,—somebody who evidently expected to enter as readily as before, and had worked ineffectually for several minutes before abandoning the attempt, and then only to be caught in the act and unblushingly to repudiate the same.

"Bayard," said the major, "I am the last man to interfere in the details of my subordinates' management of affairs, but there's a matter I want to ask you about while we are out here. What is the reason Dr. Weeks refuses to let Mrs. Miller go in and see McLean? She has been always very fond of him, and naturally wants to be of service now. Of course, if there be any good and sufficient reason, I've nothing to say, but I think I've a right to know."

Bayard hesitated a moment. "Come out here on the piazza, major," he presently said. "I don't want them to hear in the parlor." And together the two officers walked over to the wooden railing and stood there looking at each other. It was evident to the post commander in an instant that what his surgeon had to tell was something of no little importance and something, furthermore, that he shrank from mentioning. Bayard's eyes fell before the major's earnest and troubled gaze; he was plainly studying how to put his information fairly and without prejudice. Suddenly he looked up.

"First, while we are on the subject, let me finish about this latch business, major. It is not entirely— entirely irrelevant to the other matter. You see I had to tell Robert why we made such particular inquiries about the door. Now the boy has been with me for years, and came to me with a most unblemished character. Why, he was body-servant for the adjutant and quartermaster of the First Artillery in the lively old days at Fort Hamilton, and had unlimited opportunities for peculation; but those gentlemen said he was simply above suspicion. But he is sensitive, and it worried him fearfully lest Mr. Holmes should think he or some of his assistants in the kitchen had been searching those pockets. Now it was simply on his account—to convince him it was somebody from outside that surreptitiously entered the hall while we were all at dinner—that

Holmes took the trouble to test the latch, and with a little bit of stiff wire he showed us how Robert's device could be circumvented."

"And Holmes has no doubt it was so accomplished?" asked the major, tentatively.

Bayard looked embarrassed. "I cannot say just what he does think, major, because he utterly refuses to speak of it. He said it was absurd to make such an ado about nothing, and declared he would be seriously annoyed if I pursued the subject."

"But you admit you have a theory of your own?" and Miller keenly eyed his medical officer as though striving to read beneath that smooth and polished surface.

"I have what might be called an hypothesis, a vague theory, and a suspicion that would be entirely intangible but for one or two little things that have recently come to my knowledge."

"And those little things point to an inmate of the garrison, do they not?" asked Miller, with as much nonchalance as he could assume.

"I fear so," was the doctor's answer. "But you asked why Mrs. Miller was urged not to come to Mr. McLean's room just yet; that is the way Weeks put it to me when I overhauled him, which I did at the moment the matter came to my ears. Rest assured I was quite as ready to take umbrage at his action,—

more so, rather, than you could have been. But, major, could you have heard his explanation, you yourself would have been the first to say no one but his physician should be allowed to stay there. Weeks even sent the hospital nurse away, and sat up with him all night himself."

"Has he been delirious?"

"Yes, and in his delirium he has been talking of things that have completely stampeded poor Weeks. Of course he could not give me the faintest inkling of what they were, and I would not ask; but they were of such a character that they should be treated as sacred confidences, and Weeks said to me that no court-martial could drag them from his lips. He would resign first. It was for fear his patient might continue the subject in her presence that Weeks begged Mrs. Miller not to think of coming to nurse him yet awhile. He assures me that the moment the fever subsides he will be glad to have her aid, for he looks worn-out now. Were not his reasons cogent?"

Miller bowed his head. "I had not thought of this," he said; "Mrs. Miller will be as sorry as I am to hear of it, and, of course, she will appreciate the reasons. Did Weeks tell you when this delirium began?"

"The night after Hatton left, or, rather, very early in the morning of the next day. He had been alarmed at McLean's symptoms during the evening, and ordered the nurse to wake him if he saw any indications of delirium. The man came to him at three in the morning, and said the lieutenant was wild. Weeks went over at once,—and ten minutes after he got there he sent the attendant away, and shut himself up with his patient."

The major pondered a moment. "Is the man close-mouthed? Do you think he could have heard much of anything before he was sent away?"

"I know very little about him. He is a member of Captain Bruce's company and very much attached to the lieutenant; so I infer from what Weeks tells me. Even if he had heard anything that ought not to leak out, it is not likely this particular man would betray it; he would say nothing that might ever harm McLean."

"Well, no! Not McLean, perhaps. Very possibly he might not know how it would harm him to have his ravings repeated. I was thinking—I could not help thinking—that Mac had been talking about —these recent thefts in garrison."

"And there have been more than this one at our house?" asked the doctor, with concern and surprise mingled in his handsome face.

"Yes, two or three more, I regret to say, but I have not full particulars yet and cannot speak of them."

Bayard clasped his hands with one of the melodramatic gestures so peculiar to him.

"My God!" he muttered. "It was bad enough as I supposed it, but I had no idea it had come to such a pass as this."

"Bayard," said the major, after a moment of earnest thought, "this is a matter that must be handled with the utmost care and circumspection. Not a vestige of suspicion must be permitted to circulate if we can prevent it. I have strictly enjoined secrecy upon my— my informant, and I desire you to regard this talk as confidential. Tell Weeks I appreciate and sustain him in this caution and thank him for his efforts to stifle any possible scandal. Poor Mac! The youngster would be horror-stricken if he knew what secrets he had been blabbing."

"His troubles must have been weighing on his mind a long time," said the doctor, "and yet I never suspected it. I don't know that I ever saw a blither young fellow until about the time the finding of that board of survey was announced. He didn't seem to expect that at all."

"Well,—neither did I. Of course, technically it had to go against him, but we never dreamed it would result in stoppage of his pay."

"And yet his funds were all right, I'm told," said the doctor, musingly. "One would suppose that if he had any tendencies that way they would have cropped out when he had so much public money passing through his hands."

"Tendencies what way, doctor? I don't follow you."

"Why, in the way these—these little thefts and his delirious utterances would seem to indicate," said Bayard, hesitatingly.

Miller fairly sprang up from the rail on which he was leaning, his eyes distended with wonderment and pain.

"In God's name, Bayard, what are you talking about?" he gasped.

"About this sad case of McLean's, major, as I supposed you were."

"You don't mean that your theory involves him? You don't mean it—it is of himself, of his connection with these thefts, that he has been telling in his delirium?"

"Why, Major Miller, I supposed of course you understood—I—I, of course, accuse nobody, but of whom could he have been talking about but himself? That was certainly my understanding of it?"

For one moment the old major stood there looking into the staff-officer's eyes,—amaze, consternation, distress, all mingled in his florid, weather-beaten face. Then without a word he turned and stumbled away down the steps and hurried from the gate. The trim, spruce orderly, standing on the walk without, raised his gloved hand in salute and stood attention as the commanding officer passed him, then "fell in" ten paces behind and followed in his tracks. But for once in his life the major neither saw nor returned a soldier's respectful salutation.

XIV.

The fever had left him, and Randall McLean, very white and "peaked" looking, was sitting propped up in bed and enjoying the wine-jelly Mrs. Miller had brought with her own hands. She had hoped to find him in better spirits, and was distressed to see how downcast and listless he was. Just what evil spell had fallen upon the garrison Mrs. Miller could not explain. The major for two or three days had been utterly unlike himself, and would give her no good reason. The cavalry battalion that had reached the post and gone into camp down on the flats to the north was almost ready to push on toward the Black Hills, and though she had twice reminded him that he ought at least to invite the field and staff officers to dinner, her usually social spouse had declined, saying he felt utterly unequal to it. The lethargy and gloom at post "head-quarters" seemed to pervade the entire garrison. Nobody felt like doing anything to dispel it. The band played blithely enough at guard-mounting and again in the sunshiny afternoons, but nobody came out and danced on the broad piazzas as used to be the way at Laramie. Nellie Bayard was beginning to sit out on the veranda in a big easy-chair with Janet Bruce as her constant companion, and the Gordon girls, those indomitably jolly creatures, as occasional visitors; but as Miss Kate, the elder, expressed herself, "Laramie is nothing but one big hospital now. The women and children are the only able-bodied men in it." Nellie was kind and civil, and tried to be cordial to them, but they were "smart" enough to see she had no heart for rattling small talk and crisp comments on matters and things at the post, and much preferred to be left alone to her undisturbed confidential chats with "Bonnie Jean." Blunt was slowly mending, and Dr. Weeks was having a little rest after an anxious week, when his services were demanded for another patient in Bedlam,—no less a person than the queen herself.

In view of the fact that Dr. Bayard was the recognized family physician and had been and was still assiduously attending Mrs. Forrest, it was considered nothing short of an intentional slight on the young lady's part that she should send for Weeks. It was Mrs. Post who came over to Blunt's door when she knew the junior doctor was there, and asked him to come with her and see Miss Forrest. For two days the latter had been confined to her room refusing to see any physician, and declaring that in Mrs. Post's ministrations she found all the physic she needed, but now the time seemed to have come when medical aid was really necessary. Dr. Bayard's face, when he was told by Mrs. Post that Weeks was summoned and in attendance, was a study worth seeing. It was not a serious ailment at all, said Mrs. Post. Miss Forrest had caught cold and neglected it, and now the cold had developed into fever, and she had been persuaded to keep in bed for a day or two.

But Mrs. Miller was puzzled over still another matter. The evening of the day Mr. Holmes so unexpectedly reappeared at Laramie, he and Miss Forrest met on the board-walk near "Bedlam," had a few moments' conversation there just before gun-fire at retreat, and then, to the surprise of many lookers-on, she was observed to take his proffered arm, and for over half an hour they strolled around the deserted parade talking earnestly together. It was the hour when most of the garrison families were in the dining-rooms, at dinner or tea as might be the custom of the household; but more than one good lady found it necessary to pop up from the table and go to the front window to see if Mr. Holmes and Miss Forrest were still walking and talking together. It was the morning after this mysterious consultation that the cold developed; and those kindly spirits who had promptly decided that the handsome but penniless New York girl was setting her cap to cut out Nellie Bayard with the Chicago millionaire were balked in their hopes of seeing further developments by the circumstance of her keeping her room and not again meeting Mr. Holmes, who, after two or three days' visit, departed as suddenly and unexpectedly as he came. The presence of a large battalion of cavalry had the effect of warning the Indians away from the neighborhood and made travel again comparatively safe.

And now, having patted up his pillows and settled him carefully back upon them, Mrs. Miller had begun the attempt of cheering her "pet lieutenant," as the major had called him. First she strove to rouse his interest by detailing the terms in which Captain Terry had officially commended his gallantry and zeal in the fight down at Royall's Ford; but he had heard it all before through Dr. Weeks, and, though appreciative, he did not beam with the comfort she expected. Then she tried to tell him of Major Miller's warm-hearted and commendatory endorsement in forwarding Terry's report; but he had heard of that too; the adjutant had told him about it, and there was nothing new in it. What did it amount to, after all? said Mac to himself. What good result can follow? No matter how zealously a fellow may serve in the field,—no matter what dangers he may encounter, hardships he may endure, wounds he may receive, Indians he may kill or capture,—in this blessed republican land of ours the principle is too well established that promotion in the line goes only by seniority, and to the staff—like kissing—mainly by favor. Not even a "brevet," he well knew, could be won by daring conduct in action against savage foes; and, to sum the matter up in a few words, the men who stood the best chance for advancement in the army were those who studiously avoided excitement of any kind, especially that to be found in Western campaigns. They all understood this thing at Laramie just as well as he did, and therefore appreciated his soldierly conduct for what it was really worth.

"But the major thinks it may be the means of removing that stoppage against your pay, Mr. McLean," said Mrs. Miller. "Surely the general will do something to secure recognition or reward."

"I fear not, Mrs. Miller," was the doleful answer; "that is just about the last thing this government of ours is apt to do; what I've got before me is the prospect of having to live for a year or more on 'board wages,' and see my pay raked in month after month to make up for the stealings of a rascal too sharp for any of us even to suspect. It would be hard at any time, but—it's rough now, and no mistake." And poor Mac turned his head away as he spoke.

There was silence a moment. The womanly heart was touched at his despair and suffering, yet impotent to cheer him. Suddenly she bent over him as he lay there, so white and weary looking.

"Mac, don't, don't worry so. I can't bear to see you troubled. I know—I can't help knowing— what's the matter; and indeed,—indeed I think you have cause to hope rather than despair. Did you know he had gone away again?"

"Yes. Weeks told me."

"She cares nothing whatever for him. Janet Bruce is with her all the time, Mac, and she told me she almost shrank from him. Now, if he were simply her father's friend, she could not but like him. Everybody likes him, Mac, and I have reason to know what a considerate and thorough gentleman he is. But it is because he has attempted to be more that she has turned against him, and Janet says she knows he has seen it and made up his mind to accept it as final. The last two days of his visit he avoided her all the time, only conversed with her when they were unavoidably thrown together, and was then simply bright and laughing and friendly. Janet says that Nellie seemed inexpressibly relieved by the change in his manner. Come, old fellow, cheer up and get well, and let us have you out in the sunshine a day or two, and then we'll see if a few long talks with her won't help matters. She's a child yet, and almost too young to fall in love with anybody. You know she has seen next to nothing of the world."

"That is just what stings and torments me so, Mrs. Miller," answered McLean, with unexpected energy. "That is what weighs upon my heart and soul. She has seen very little of the world. She is young, inexperienced, and motherless. Her father does not like me, and I know it, and simply because he saw my deep interest in her, and, having other views, he was determined to break it off in the bud. What possible right have I—poor, friendless, utterly without position or influence, saddled with this mountain of uncontracted debt—to seek to win such a girl as she for my wife? What have I to offer but misfortune and trouble? No, Mrs. Miller, it is all useless. If I have stood between her and such a future as he could offer her, God forgive me. I did not know the millstone that was to be hung about my neck. I did not dream of his existence. I just drifted in, and now I could pray heaven she hasn't."

Again he turned away, with something very like a sob in his weak voice, and buried his face in his arm.

"Mac," she persisted, "I'm not going to sit here and see you accusing yourself of wrong-doing in this way. Let me tell you that if she does care for you, and I believe she does, Nellie Bayard would rather be your wife in one room and a kitchen than live in opulence in New York or Chicago. What's more, she would wait for you loyally, faithfully, until you were thoroughly on your feet again, with this debt paid and a little laid by. As for Dr. Bayard's plans for her, he is worldly enough, of course, to seek such wealth as Roswell Holmes's for his daughter; but the man himself is changing his mind. You should have seen him devoting himself to Miss Forrest out here one evening. Now, there's a girl who would appreciate his money and spend it for him like a duchess."

But McLean was silent.

"Did you get to know her at all well?" asked Mrs. Miller presently.

"Very slightly indeed."

"And yet, living in the same building with her, as you and Mr. Hatton did, I fancied you would see her quite frequently."

"I didn't. I believe Hat did."

"Yes—his rooms being up-stairs, and opening on that gallery where she used to promenade so much, it was natural that he should see more of her. It worried Jeannie Bruce not a little. I never knew whether she cared for Mr. Hatton or not until Miss Forrest took to parading up and down in front of his rooms."

"Hat says she never came as far as his window. She turned about before she reached the hall-door always."

"Tell me, Mac. Do you think Mr. Hatton liked her?"

McLean's pale face flushed a little. He felt that questions were trembling on her lips which he did not wish to answer, and the one thing he could not do was equivocate.

"I'd rather you'd wait and ask him," he finally said.

"Oh! I don't mean as he likes Janet Bruce; what I meant was—well, you or he or both of you —did you feel that you—well—trusted her?"

McLean fairly squirmed in his nest under the sheets. This was just the drift he had dreaded. How he wished Weeks would come in and tell her they were talking too much and would be sure to throw him into a fever again, but no Weeks was to be had; he had gone home for a rest, and probably would not appear again until afternoon. He glanced uneasily into the front room.

"No! The hospital attendant is not there, Mac. I sent him off on an errand. You need not be afraid of his hearing,—and, besides, he has heard you talk about her. I thought you ought to know."

"Has heard me talk about her,—Miss Forrest? What on earth do you mean, Mrs. Miller?" And now he had turned toward her, his face filled with anxiety and alarm.

"Don't worry, Mac. I found it out instantly. You know he is a married man, and his wife has been my laundress for over five years. You talked about her when you were delirious,—not very much,—nothing —nothing I did not already know; but Dr. Weeks turned him away and took care of you from the moment Lachlan went for him and told him you were talking wild, and of course his wife wormed out of him why he was not needed for two days, and, little by little, what you had said. Luckily she came right to me, and I put a stopper on her tongue."

"My God! My God! What have I done?" moaned McLean, as he threw his arm over his eyes. "What did I say? What have I revealed, Mrs. Miller? I must know."

"Nothing; again I assure you, nothing that we— that is—I—did not already have good cause to suspect and know. It came to me from Robinson, Mac, before you dreamed of anything of the kind, so you are in no wise responsible. She must have a mania, there's no other explanation for it; but we're going to keep it all quiet. No one is to know until Captain Forrest gets back at the end of the campaign. Then he will be told, and restitution be made. But isn't it dreadful?"

For all answer McLean would only shake his head. He was stunned—horrified at thought of the wild revelation he had made. He could not bear to speak of it. Yet now he felt that he must know how much he had let fall.

"It is the last time that fellow Lachlan shall enter this room," he muttered between his teeth. "I'll have Weeks send him back to his company this very day."

"No, don't blame Lachlan. The poor fellow meant no harm. He only told it as evidence of the extremity of your delirium. He does not dream the truth with regard to her, though I fear his wife does. Why, Mac, if they had not come away from Robinson when they did, the whole post would have been in an uproar. Things were disappearing all the time,— money and valuables,—and since they left there it has all stopped, but has begun here. You and Mr. Hatton are not the only losers. Mr. Holmes confessed to me that his porte-monnaie had been stolen from his fur overcoat the night we were there at the doctor's, and I saw her standing by it, patting it and pretending to admire it; and I know that she has been sending registered letters away, and that bills are constantly coming to her from the East. Mrs. Griffin told me so. And then Mr. Hatton—well, you know he has confided in me in ever so many things—he told me a good deal before he went away. No, indeed, Mac. It isn't that you have revealed anything I did not know. It is only that I felt you ought to be told of it."

But McLean could not be comforted. "Who else knows of this?" he presently asked.

"I have told the major. We had talked it all over before your illness. Mrs. Bruce knows, for she too gets letters from Robinson. And perhaps there are one or two who suspect, but that is all. Mr. Hatton is the one who knows most about it all, and has most reason to believe in her guilt. When did you become convinced?"

"I don't know,—that night Hatton told me, I suppose,—the night the major came to see me, and Hatton begged off. You know about it?"

"The major told me he had gone to see you about some evidence you had; Mr. Hatton met him at the door and explained that you were asleep. Was that the night you mean, Mr. McLean? Was that the night that you became convinced that she was the thief?"

"That was the night."

"But what happened then to convince you? I ought to know. It is far better that I should know than have this cruel half belief."

"I—Mrs. Miller, forgive me, but it is a matter I cannot speak of. Hatton and I 'shook hands' on it we would say nothing to any one of our knowledge, and I cannot speak of it. Wait until he returns. He ought to be back to-morrow. You know he only went with the guard to the stockade up on Sage Creek. It's only three days' march. If he will tell you, well and good; but I will not say anything more,—just now, at any rate."

There came a quick step along the wooden piazza without, a tap at the door, and Dr. Weeks peered in. Glancing over her shoulder, Mrs. Miller saw that his face was white,—that he was beckoning to her; and she presently arose and went into the front room. She heard hoof-beats passing the house at a rapid trot. She heard hurrying feet and excited voices, and then the young doctor stretched forth his hand at the doorway and led her into the hall.

"Stay with McLean as much as you can, and keep this from him if possible. A courier is just in who got through, God knows how, during the night. Hatton and his party were corralled yesterday beyond Rawhide Butte. Several of them are killed already. The cavalry start at once, and I go with them."

XV.

For a man who prided himself on the ease and self-possession which made him so distinguished a feature in society, Dr. Bayard could not but confess to himself that the sudden orders which sent his assistant away left him in a somewhat embarrassing position. The care of Weeks's patients now devolved upon the senior, and among these patients was one who much needed his attention, but whom he shrank from seeing, —Randall McLean,—and another whom he greatly desired to attend, but who shrank from seeing him,—Miss Forrest.

Mrs. Miller was still at the bedside of the former when Dr. Bayard nerved himself to make the necessary call. To his great relief, the young soldier had fallen into a fitful doze and was unconscious of his presence. Mrs. Miller, in low tones, described his condition; and the doctor was content to go without other examination, though he left directions with the attendant as to what was to be done when the patient awaked. Next he repaired to Mrs. Forrest's rooms, and was measurably soothed and flattered by her appreciative reception. He bade her pay no attention to the rumors rushing through the post, and dinned into

her affrighted ears by Celestine, as to the probable fate
of Hatton and his little command. He pointed out
to her, as he had to other ladies whom he had been
summoned to attend that gruesome afternoon, that it
was not the first time Mr. Hatton had been "corralled" by the Sioux, and that he had always successfully kept them at respectful distance, and his own
command under cover, until the rescuers in shape of
cavalry could reach the scene. It is true that in this
instance the attack seemed to have been fierce and
sudden, and the courier gave the names of two men
who were killed instantly; but, said he, as that attack
was repelled, and Hatton lost no time in getting his
men into a little hollow, he believed and Major Miller
believed that they could "stand off" the Indians in-
definitely. The cavalry would certainly reach them
early in the morning, and that would be the end of it.
Forty-two hours wasn't very long compared with
other sieges those infantrymen had sustained in escort-
ing trains through the Indian country, and, if they
only had water for their wounded, all would go well.
There was the main trouble, said the doctor. What
with the Niobrara and the Rawhide and the little
streams running into them, and the spring at Box
Elder, close to the road, there was so much water
along the route that possibly they had neglected to fill
the barrel on their wagon and the canteen carried by

each man. If that were the case, and the Indians had surrounded them some distance from any spring or stream, then the wounded might, indeed, have to suffer a day or so, but he anticipated nothing worse. He had talked it all over with Miller before setting forth on his rounds, and knew just what to say. Most women were reassured and rendered hopeful, but Mrs. Forrest's spirits were at low ebb and she required consolation in double allowance. Bayard lingered with her, nothing loath, hoping that Miss Forrest might come into the family sitting-room to hear his version of affairs at the front. Even after Mrs. Forrest was talked out, and the font of her ready tears was nearly pumped dry, he held his ground, examining Maud's and Vickie's juvenile tongues and dandling baby Hal to that youngster's keen delight. But no one came along the hall whose step sounded like hers, and at last his patience gave out.

"And how is Miss Forrest this afternoon?" he asked.

"Still confined to her room and bed, doctor, but she says she means to get up and dress this evening. Now, do you think it prudent for her to go out in the night air?"

"On general principles, Mrs. Forrest," answered the doctor, slowly and impressively, "I should say no, but I have no knowledge of the merits of this case. You will remember that my services were virtually declined by the young lady in favor of those of the assistant."

"I know, doctor, I know. Fanny is simply the most incomprehensible creature I ever met. I cannot understand her at all, and it's useless for me to talk to her. I told her that you were the family physician, and pointed out to her that a simple regard for the proprieties ought to show her how much better it would be to call you instead of a gentleman so much younger; but she pays no attention to anything I say. She never has."

Bayard winced not a little at the invidious comparison on the score of age, but, now that the subject was opened, he desired to "prospect" a little. There was another view to be taken, and one far more flattering to his *amour propre*. Probably, in the coyness of a woman who had recognized the lover in his looks and language, Miss Forrest had tacitly admitted his claim to be regarded as such by summoning another, not a lover, to attend her professionally. If this hypothesis proved correct he would have some grounds for hope. Two things, however, he greatly desired to know before taking the plunge. First, was it possible that Mr. Courtlandt proposed leaving her a lump of his large fortune? Second, was it possible that she had already given her heart to another? He well knew that on neither point would Miss Forrest be confidential with so weak a vessel as her sister-in-law; but, on the other hand,—and the doctor reasoned well,—he felt sure that, in order to reconcile her to having Fanny as an inmate of their household, Captain Forrest had been compelled to tell her why he had withdrawn his sister from such luxurious surroundings in New York and brought her to share his humble fare as a soldier on the far frontier. He had heard from a dozen sources how Forrest had almost painfully truckled to his querulous wife; always pleading, explaining, conciliating; always fearful of saying or doing, or leaving unsaid or undone, something, the doing or neglecting of which was sure to wound her sensitive soul and bring on a flood of tears and reproaches. "If she were my wife," said blunt old Bruce, "I'd pack her off home to that doting father she's always prating about, and I'd keep her there until she arrived at years of discretion. It is simply pitiful to see a big, stalwart, soldierly fellow like Forrest led around by the nose like a ringed bull by that ridiculous and lackadaisical creature." Beyond doubt there would have been far more happiness all around if Forrest had firmly set down his foot and refused to be longer the victim of her whims and caprices. There would doubtless have been a few days of sore lamentation and despairing appeals to be restored to her father's arms (where she was not at all wanted, that estimable ecclesiastic having only recently taken thereto a successor to her sainted mother); but in the end she would have respected him far more and been happier in obeying him. Like many another husband, poor Forrest was at times conscious of his duty in the case; but, like most others, shrank from the ordeal. Bruce himself, so savagely critical of the weakness of other spouses, was notoriously subservient to the wishes of Mrs. Bruce; but she never had to resort to tears to accomplish her object, and was thoroughly in unison with her husband in his condemnation of Forrest's weakness. "Poor, poor fellow!" she was saying to herself this very day. "With such a fool for a wife and such a—such a sharper for a sister!"

So confident was Bayard of his ground that he had decided, days since, on his plan of attack. He would not ask direct questions, for her husband had doubtless pledged her to secrecy. He would delicately but unhesitatingly speak of Miss Forrest as though he had full knowledge of her past, and he felt assured that he could read in the patient's face, even in the unlikely event of her silence, whether or no his theories were correct. Besides, he had ventured an inquiry or two of an old New York associate and club-fellow, a man who had known the Courtlandts well.

"We must not judge Miss Forrest harshly, dear lady," he soothingly remarked, after a moment of deep thought and apparent hesitation. "I confess that I felt a little aggrieved at first when she saw fit to summon Dr. Weeks despite the fact that I was in the house as your physician two or three times a day; but, after thinking it all over, her motives were apparent and—quite natural. You probably did not know that I was well acquainted with Mr. Courtlandt, did you?"

"No! were you?" asked Mrs. Forrest, with dilating eyes. "And Fanny knew,—and did not tell me——"

"Yes. We were members of the same club, and I used to see a great deal of him before coming West." It was very long before, and it was only seeing, but Bayard did not care to explain this. He wished to convey the idea that his acquaintance with the old gentleman had been recent and confidential, and he succeeded.

"How strange that you should be here—where she is. I'm sure Captain Forrest has no idea of it, doctor. Did—did you ever speak with her about—the Courtlandts?"

"Yes, once. Of course she did not care to talk of

the matter at first. It was only when she found that I knew Mr. Courtlandt so well, that she became at all communicative."

"And did she talk of her affair—of Mr. Courtlandt —the younger one I mean?"

"My dear Mrs. Forrest! We could hardly expect a young lady to be communicative on such a topic as that. Of course there were some things I could not help knowing, and that is why I say we ought not to judge her harshly now. Her experience of last year was not calculated to make a girl look upon the world with kindlier eyes, and the contrast between the life she leads now and that she led under her kinsman's roof is enough to dishearten any woman."

"I'm sure I do everything I possibly can to make her content and happy," impetuously exclaimed Mrs. Forrest. "And it's all her own fault if she isn't. She—she needn't have come at all. Mr. Courtlandt told her and told Captain Forrest that it should make no difference; but she is self-willed and obstinate, and nothing would do but she must quit his roof forever and come to be a burden on her brother, who has quite enough to stagger under already." ("Hum!" thought Bayard at this juncture, "how little she realizes the truth of that assertion!") "Mr. Courtlandt had been devoted to her from her childhood, had lavished everything on her, had educated her, sent her abroad, provided for her in every way, and—she rewarded him by taking this silly prejudice against his son, whom she ought to have had sense enough to know he expected her to marry."

Bayard's pulse gave a leap, but his fine face made no sign. Professional imperturbability alone expressed itself. She paused one instant for breath. Then it occurred to her that perhaps she was broadly trenching on forbidden ground and revealing that which her husband had bidden her keep inviolate. Bayard read her like an open book, and promptly took the initiative before she could question.

"And yet, Mrs. Forrest, would you have had her—a woman of such superior attainments and character—would your husband have had her marry a man to whom she could not look up?—whose character and, pardon me, whose habits were so, let us say, unsettled?"

"Then she ought to have left before. I know she says she never dreamed of its being her uncle's plan or hope,—never dreamed that the young man was in earnest. It was all nonsense to say she couldn't marry a man whom she did not look up to and respect. He is only a year younger than she is, and lots of girls marry men younger than themselves,—especially when such a fortune was involved. Why! Mr. Courtlandt would have left them everything he had in the world, if she would only have consented."

"But women form their own ideals, dear lady, and she may have had a man in view whom she did look up to, honor, and love. Is not that a reasonable theory?" And the doctor's eyes, full of sympathy and deference, watched his impulsive patient narrowly withal. How well he knew her! She fell instantly into the trap.

"But she hadn't! I could forgive her easily if that were so, but she told the captain it was purely and simply that she could not and would not marry Philip Courtlandt or any man like him."

"But I fancied from what—from various circumstances—that the young man was very dissipated—dangerously so, in fact. Would you counsel your sister to marry such a man?"

"Well, why not? He has been wild, I know. My husband looked into the whole case, and, of course, he sustains her. Phil Courtlandt had to go into a retreat once, but I believe it was because she treated him so. His father was sure that she could reform and make a man of him, and he almost implored her to take pity on his gray hairs and save his boy. I tell you I think it was sheer ingratitude. Even if she couldn't have reformed him, there would have been all that money." And Mrs. Forrest sighed pathetically at thought of the thousands her hard-headed, hard-hearted sister had refused. Bayard, congratulating himself on his success thus far, had still another point on which he desired information,—a vital point.

"What seems so bad about the whole matter," he said, after a sympathetic echo of the lady's sigh, "is the disappointment of old Mr. Courtlandt. No doubt, despite their cousinship, this has long been his cherished scheme; and it must make him—at least I do not wonder that it makes him a trifle bitter against her."

"Why, doctor, that is one of the queerest things to me! One would suppose that any girl of ordinary gratitude would try and repay and appreciate such devotion as has been lavished on her. She simply repels people who try to be loving to her. I'm sure I've tried every way in my power. Of course, at first he was very bitter and said some severe things,—at least she so told Captain Forrest,—but she has no right to treasure them up against him. He said he had reared and educated and cherished her purposely to be the salvation of his wayward son, and, as she would not have the son, she said she could not live under his roof. Then he had always given her a liberal allowance, besides paying the most extraordinary bills, and she hurt him fearfully—I know she did—by refusing to accept it afterward. He has sent it to her even here, and she almost hurls it back at him,—and here are Maud and Vickie without a decent dress to their names," wailed Mrs. Forrest in somewhat irrelevant conclusion, and the tears welled again from her weary eyes.

Bayard was again silent a moment, waiting for his patient to recover her composure and her tongue. It was comfort to think that, at least, Mr. Courtlandt's munificence was still a fact. But how about the future?

"Anything that might tend to widen the breach between them would, of course, be deplorable," he presently said; "but I infer, from the fact that he continues to send her allowance to her, that he will be apt to provide liberally for her in his will."

"He would do anything for her, I've no doubt, despite her ingratitude; but she has told Captain Forrest that after what has passed she cannot and will not accept a penny from him. Now what can one say to a girl like that?"

And this question the doctor could not answer. After a few moments' thought, he arose as if to go.

"I am heartily glad to know that she is so much better this afternoon. These are anxious days for us all, and it is not to be wondered at that so many of our ladies are prostrated. Will you kindly say to her that I called to inquire after her, and am rejoiced to think we will soon be able to welcome her out again?

And, Mrs. Forrest, you might say to her that it would gladden my little girl if she would come over and sit with her or sing to her. Elinor has been very low-spirited to-day, owing, no doubt, to the fact that Jeannie Bruce has been in tears much of the time since Hatton left. Good-afternoon, Mrs. Forrest. Good-by, little ones." And the courtly doctor took his leave.

As he descended the stairs with characteristic deliberation and dignity, Celestine came forth from the dining-room and met him at the foot of the stairs.

"Mr. Holmes is come, doctor," she said, showing her white teeth. "Specks he'll be glad to find Miss Nellie sittin' up again. T'warn't no use 'n Miss Fanny t' try to catch him, 'n' I told her so when she was writin' to him. He's out yahnder along with Major Miller now."

And though the doctor frowned majestically and strode by the gabbling hussy without a word, it gave him an uncomfortable start to hear her words. What had happened that Fanny Forrest should be writing now to Roswell Holmes? This was something to be looked into.

XVI.

It was nearly two days before authentic news came in from the Niobrara, where Hatton's little command had been "corralled." Just as at first reported, the Indians in overwhelming numbers had suddenly charged down upon the detachment from behind a ridge that lay full half a mile to the east of the road; while others, crouching in a dry watercourse, had picked off the leading soldiers,—the two men thrown out to the front to scout the trail and secure the main body against surprise. Hatton, all told, had only twenty men, and the fall of the two far in the advance had for an instant flurried their comrades back at the wagons. There was no time to run these lumbering vehicles, empty though they were, into the familiar, old "prairie fort," in square or circle; but, while some of the teamsters sprang from their saddles and took refuge under their wagons, others seized their arms and joined the soldiers in a sharp fire upon the charging and yelling warriors, with the usual effect of compelling them to veer and wheel and scamper away, still keeping up a lively fusillade of their own. One mule team and wagon went tearing off full tilt across the prairie pursued by a score of jeering, laughing, and exultant braves, and was finally "rounded up" and captured by them a mile away to the west; and Hatton had promptly availed himself of the episode to make a rush with his entire party for a little hillock three hundred yards east of the road. He had marked the spot before and knew its possibilities for defence, and there in less than five minutes he had his men sheltered in an oval "dip" along the crest and yet commanding the approaches in every direction. From here they not only successfully "stood off" every attack until dark, but prevented the Indians reaching the bodies of the slain and securing the coveted trophy of their scalps, and covered the teamsters who were sent down to unhitch and secure the mules. When night came a half-breed scout slipped away with news of the "corral," and Hatton found that two of his men were severely wounded and that few of them had any water in their canteens. The river was full six miles to the south. Neither stream nor spring was close at hand, and with characteristic improvidence the teamsters had failed to fill their water-barrels at the stockade before starting. "What was the use, with the Niobrara only a few hours' march away?" Bitterly did Hatton reproach himself for his neglect in having left so important a matter to the men themselves, but there was no sense in fretting over the past. Something had to be done at once to provide water for the morrow's siege. They heard the exultant whoops of the savages, who, under cover of the darkness, had crept out and succeeded in scalping the two dead soldiers. They knew that very soon the Indians would be crawling out to the wagons in an attempt to run them away or fire them. Hatton himself ventured down to examine the water-barrels, and found not more than half a barrel of dirty, brackish, ill-flavored fluid in all. The darkness grew black and impenetrable. Heavy clouds overspread the heavens, and a moaning wind crept out of the mountain-passes of the Big Horn range and came sweeping down across the treeless prairie. Every now and then they could hear the galloping beat of pony-hoofs, and knew that they were closely invested in their hillock citadel, and at last, about ten o'clock, a sergeant who had been sent with a couple of men to see what was going on at the wagons, came running back breathless. The wagons were gone! Every one of them had been run off by the Indians under cover of the wind and darkness; and presently, half a mile over to the south-east, a glare of flame arose, and the white tops became for a moment visible, and dancing, capering naked forms around them, and then the cotton duck attracted the eager, fiery tongues, and in another moment the flames seemed to leap high in the air, but the performers in the aboriginal ballet scurried for shelter. The soldiers sighted their rifles for nine hundred yards, and the little hill blazed and sputtered half a minute with a rapid discharge that sent leaden messengers whistling through the burning wagon-covers and humming about the ears of the revellers.

Fifteen minutes later, Hatton resolved on a bold move. Mounting his wounded men on mules, and leading his little party, soldiers, teamsters, and quadrupeds, he slipped away from the hillock, and, keeping well to the east of the road, groped through the darkness back to the high range overlooking the valleys of "Old Woman's Fork" of the South Cheyenne and Hat Creek to the eastward; and morning found him bivouacked at a little spring not ten miles from the stockade. Thither, of course, the Indians trailed and followed at daybreak. There again they attacked and besieged and were repulsed, again and again; and there at dawn on the second day, after an all-night march, the trumpets of the cavalry rang the signal of rescue, and the charging troopers sent the Sioux whirling in scattered bands over the bold and beautiful upland. The little detachment was safe, but its brave commander was prostrate with a rifle-bullet through the thigh and another in the shoulder. Dr. Weeks declared it impossible to attempt to move him back to Laramie; and in a litter made with lariats and saddle-blankets the men carried their wounded leader back to the stockade at the head of Sage Creek, and there, wrote Weeks, he might have to remain a month, and there, unless otherwise ordered, the other wounded men would remain with him, Weeks himself attending them in his improvised field-hospital.

Major Miller and Dr. Bayard, after brief consultation, had decided that the young surgeon's ideas were sound. The stockade was well guarded and provisioned. Medical and surgical supplies were promptly forwarded under strong cavalry escort, and that same day the entire cavalry battalion struck its tents and moved away northward over the route Hatton had taken. Once more was Laramie left with only a handful of men and hardly a company officer for duty.

Old Bruce turned out, despite his rheumatics, and announced that he was game for any garrison service under the circumstances. Roswell Holmes, who had stowed a box of wine and several boxes of cigars in the supply-wagons, with his compliments to Dr. Weeks and his patients, and who had remained at Laramie instead of going to the front solely because of an odd turn in local events, now declared that he must be considered a brevet second lieutenant, and besought Dr. Bayard's permission to visit his patient, Mr. McLean, to solicit the loan of his uniforms, sword, etc. Major Miller laughed gleefully at the idea, and all the garrison was beginning to pluck up heart again, for Hatton's wounds were pronounced not dangerous, though painful, and all the infantry people were proud of the way he and McLean had upheld the honor of their corps. Jeannie Bruce and Elinor had had long hours of who knows what delicious confidence and tearful exchange of sympathy. McLean was reported doing very well; Blunt was improving; Miss Forrest was taking the air on the gallery. Everybody seemed in better spirits, despite a certain constraint and mystery that overhung the garrison,—everybody, with one exception—Dr. Bayard.

"Mr. McLean is improving so rapidly that he is able to sit up already and will need his uniform himself," was his response to Holmes's laughing suggestion, but both Major Miller and the gentleman addressed looked at the speaker in surprise. One might have hazarded the assertion that it was a matter of regret to the post surgeon that his patient was on the mend. Miller eyed him narrowly. Ever since the strange conversation held with the doctor, the post commander had become almost distrustful of his motives. What could he mean by intimating that McLean was the guilty party in these recent mysterious larcenies? What could have put such ideas into his head? For the first time in several days the major was tempted to reopen the subject which he had practically forbidden his wife to mention again. He longed to know what she would say or think if she knew that the surgeon was trying to divert suspicion from Miss Forrest to the wounded and unsuspecting officer. Now that the cavalry had gone out to the front and more troops were marching up from the railway, all anxiety as to his immediate surroundings was dispelled, and the major could not avoid drifting back to the strange complications in which two of the prominent people of his military bailiwick were involved. He had taken a great liking to Mr. Holmes, and had striven to open the way for that gentleman in case he had the faintest inclination to speak of his losses; but, though the civilian instantly saw what the simple-minded old soldier was aiming at, he changed the subject, and it presently became plain to the commander that he would not speak about the matter at all. Miller could not well seek his advice without telling of the other thefts of which he believed Mr. Holmes to know nothing, and yet he felt that as commanding officer it was his duty to say to the visitor how much he regretted the occurrence and how earnestly he was striving to discover the offender. But Holmes would not give him a chance. He was doing a little ferreting on his own account.

As for the doctor, two things had conspired to make him blue and unhappy. Miss Forrest was up and out on her gallery, as has been said, but was never in her sister's room when the doctor called; declined his professional services with courteous thanks and the assurance that no physician was necessary, yet begged to be excused when he sent a message by Celestine asking if she would not see him. Then he wrote her a note, and, remembering her antipathy to the mulatto girl, he sent it by Robert, charging him to take it to her door if she was not in the sitting-room, but to deliver it in person and wait for an answer. Robert found her promenading with Mrs. Post on the upper gallery, and people who had been saying that Mrs. Post had nothing to do with her at Robinson were surprised at the growing intimacy between them now. Robert presented the note with a grave and courtly Virginia bow, then withdrew to a little distance and respectfully awaited her answer. Over at the Gordons' a group of ladies, old and young, watched the scene with curious and speculative eyes. Everybody knew that Miss Forrest had declined to see Dr. Bayard during her illness. Everybody had noted that, while the entire feminine element of the garrison flocked to inquire for Nellie in her invalid state, nobody went to see Fanny Forrest. Now, what could this strange girl be doing with letters from "Dr. Chesterfield"? Even Mrs. Post watched her narrowly as she hurriedly read the lines of the doctor's elegant missive. Her eyes seemed to dilate, her color heightened and a little frown set itself darkly on her brow; but she looked up brightly after a moment's thought, and spoke kindly and pleasantly to the waiting messenger,—

"There is no answer, at least not now, Robert. Thank the doctor and tell him I am very much better."

And so, empty-handed, he returned to his master, who waited expectant in his study. The message was almost an affront,—such was his pride and self-esteem; and for nearly an hour he sat there pondering over the strange characteristics of the girl who, despite the story of her poverty and dependence, had so fascinated him. It cut him to the quick that she should so avoid him, when he knew well that between her and Mr. Holmes there had been an exchange of notes. Mr. Holmes had seen fit to preserve a mysterious silence as to this significant circumstance, and finally, apparently by appointment, Mr. Holmes had called at Bedlam the evening after his arrival, and had enjoyed a long and uninterrupted conversation with Miss Forrest out on the upper gallery. Now what did this portend? It was Celestine who gave him this very interesting information as he entered the lower hall, and, despite his repellant mien, that enterprising domestic was sufficiently a judge of character to venture on a low and confidential tone of voice in addressing him. He had scowled malignantly at her and had bidden her hold her peace as he passed her by, but Celestine was in no wise dismayed. She knew her man. It was on his return from his visit that he sent his note, and then, in the gloom and silence of his library, pondered over the palpable rebuff. Over across the hall he could hear the soft voices of his daughter and her now intimate friend Jean. They were cooing and murmuring together in some girlish confidences which he was in no mood to appreciate, and with which he could feel no sympathy whatever. Then in came Holmes from the sunshine of the parade; and he heard him cheerily enter the parlor, and in hearty, cordial tones announce that he had just come from Mr. McLean's room, that that young gentleman was doing finely, and would be able to sit out on the piazza in a day or two, and that Mrs. Miller was nursing him like a mother. For a time the chat went blithely on, Jeannie Bruce and Holmes being the principals, and then came a message which called that young lassie homeward.

Presently Bayard heard the manly voice growing deeper and softer. The words were indistinguishable, but there was no misjudging the tone, such was the tremor of tenderness of every syllable. Faint, far between, and monosyllabic were Nellie's replies, but soon the father knew she was answering through her tears. It did not last long. Holmes came to the hall, turned and spoke once more to her,—no touch of reproach, no tinge of pleading, but with a ring of manly sympathy and protecting care in every word; Bayard could not but hear one sentence: "It makes me only more firmly your friend, little girl,—and his, too." And then he strode forth into the breeze and sunshine again, and no man who met him knew that he had tempted his fate and lost. Something had told him, days before, that Miss Forrest's words were prophetic, —Nellie Bayard would prefer one nearer her own years.

It was to satisfy himself that Randall McLean was that enviable somebody that he had sought this interview; and, though she had admitted nothing and he had not questioned, he had read in her tears and blushes a truth that only recently had she tremblingly admitted to herself. Now he saw his way clearly to the end.

But to Bayard the abrupt close of the murmured interview meant a possibility that filled him with double dismay. That one hope should be dashed to earth this morning was an evil sufficient unto the day. That it should be followed by the conviction that his daughter had utterly declined to consider this wealthy and most estimable gentleman as a suitor for her hand was a bitter, bitter disappointment; but that she should have refused Roswell Holmes, with all his advantages, because of Randall McLean—with what?—was more than he could bear.

Just as she was hurrying to her room, still weeping, he interposed.

"My little Nell!—my precious!" he cried, in tenderest tones, as he folded her in his arms. "Is it so hopeless as this? Is it possible that my little daughter's heart has been stolen away—right under my eyes—and I never saw it?"

For an answer she only clung to him, hiding her bonny face, weeping the more violently. Speak she could not.

"Nell! Nellie!" he pleaded, "try and tell me, dear. You don't know what it means to me! You don't know what fears your silence causes me! My child—tell me—that it isn't Mr. McLean."

No answer—only closer nestling; only added tears.

"Nell, my own little one! If you knew with what awful dread I waited! If you knew what this meant to me—to you—to us all! Speak to me, daughter. Tell me it isn't that unhappy young man."

And now, startled, shocked, she lifts her brimming eyes in wonderment to her father's face, gazing at him through the mist of tears.

"Why unhappy?" she almost gasps. "Why—why not Mr. McLean, papa?"

For a moment Bayard stands as though stunned. Then slowly relaxes the clasp of his arms and turns drearily away, covering his face with his hands.

"My God!" he moans. "This is retribution, this is punishment! Blinder than the veriest mole have I been through it all. Nellie!" he cries, turning suddenly toward her again as she stands there trembling at his melodramatic misery. "There is no engagement! There has been nothing said, has there? Tell me!"

"Not a word,—from me," she whispers low. "He sent me a little note yesterday through Jeannie. Indeed, you can see it, papa; but I have not answered. It doesn't ask anything."

"Then promise me no word shall go, my child! Promise me! I cannot tell you why just yet, but he is not the man to whom I could ever consent to give you. My child! my child! his name is clouded; his honor is tarnished; he stands accused of crime. Nellie —my God! you must hear it sooner or later."

But now she draws away from him and leans upon the balusters, looking into his face as though she doubted his sanity.

"Father!" she slowly speaks at length, "I could no more believe such a thing of him—than I could of you."

A quick, springy step is suddenly heard on the wooden walk without, the rattle of an infantry sword against the steps, an imperative rat-tat-tat at the door. Elinor speeds away to hide her flushed cheeks and tearful eyes in the solitude of her room. Bayard quickly composes his features to their conventional calm and recedes to the gloom of the library. Robert majestically stalks through the hall and opens the door.

"Dr. Bayard in?" asks the brusque voice of the adjutant. "Ah, doctor," continues that officer, marching straightway into the den, "Major Miller is at the gate and on his way to visit Mr. McLean. He begs that you will be present at the interview, as it is on a matter of much importance."

"Very well, Mr. Adjutant," answers Bayard, gravely, as though divining the solemn import of their errand. "I am at your service at once."

XVII.

An odd despatch was that which went by the single wire of the military telegraph line to Fort Fetterman late that night. It was known that a small escort would leave that point early in the morning, going through with a staff-officer *en route* to join the field column now busily engaging the hostile Indians along the northern foot-hills of the Big Horn range. Major Miller asked the commanding officer at Fetterman to hold back a brace of horsemen to await the arrival of a courier just leaving Laramie, and bearing an important and confidential letter to the general commanding the department, who was with his troops in the field. It was over eighty miles by the river road; the night was dark and the skies overcast. There might be Indians along the route; there certainly were no soldiers, for, with the exception of eight or ten men, all of Captain Terry's troop were with him scouting on the north side of the Platte and over near the Sioux reservations. All the same, a single trooper, armed only with the revolver and unburdened by the usual blankets and field kit,—riding almost as light as a racer,—was to make the run and reach Fetterman the next afternoon.

This was the result of the interview with Lieutenant McLean, a conference at which were present Major and Mrs. Miller, Dr. Bayard, and the adjutant. Why Mrs. Miller, the wife of the commanding officer, should have been present in any capacity, it is not the province of the narrator to defend. She had been assiduously nursing and caring for the young officer in his weak and wounded condition. She had him where he could not escape her shrewd and relentless questionings. She was enabled to tell him much that Hatton had told her and a few things she certainly thought he had and therefore said he had. She was further enabled to tell him of the letters from Robinson and all they portended; of Mr. Holmes's loss and what she had seen in the mirror; of her own meeting with Miss Forrest in the darkness of the doctor's hall; of the registered letters sent away when everybody knew Mrs. Forrest hadn't a penny except the captain's pay, and that she had openly and repeatedly announced that her sister-in-law had now come to be a burden, too, having quarrelled with her relatives in the East. And so, little by little, she had drawn from McLean the story of Hatton's farewell words and the discovery of the card in the handkerchief. Then, fortified with this intelligence, and firmly convinced that she could not be mistaken in the guilt of her Majesty of Bedlam, Mrs. Miller reopened the subject and prodded the major into immediate action. She meant well. She intended no public exposure, no unnecessary disgrace. She merely wanted that Captain Forrest should come at once, compel his much-afflicted sister (for, of course, kleptomania was the sole explanation) to make restitution, and then remove her to some safe retreat in the distant East. Miller decided to see McLean at once, taking his adjutant to jot down the statements made, and Dr. Bayard because of his rank in the service and his professional connection with the officer in question. Mrs. Miller decided to be present because of McLean's great reluctance to tell what he knew and because she conceived it her duty to prompt him; and this was the quartet that swooped down upon the poor fellow in his defenceless condition late that sunshiny afternoon. No wonder his recovery was delayed!

The most stunned and bewildered man of the party while the painful interview was in progress was Dr. Bayard. He had gone in the confident expectation that McLean was to be confronted with the evidences of his guilt, and offered the chance of immediate resignation. His patient was sufficiently removed from the danger-line to enable him to sustain the shock, and he had not interposed. It was too late, therefore, to put an end to matters on that plea when to his horror-stricken ears was revealed the evidence against the woman who had so enthralled and piqued him. Miller led him away in a semi-dazed condition after the close of the conference, and then at last the doctor's vehement emotions found tongue.

"And all this time you have been suspecting that poor young fellow!" said the major, with a touch of reproach in his voice.

There was silence an instant. The doctor stopped short and leaned against the fence in front of the adjutant's quarters, his face purpling with wrath and indignation, his lips twitching, his hands clinched. Miller looked at him in amaze, and then came the outburst:

"Suspect him! By heaven, sir! What it was before is nothing to what I feel now! That in his depravity he should have stolen was bad enough; but that now, to cover his tracks, he should accuse and defame a defenceless woman is infamy! Look at his story, and tell me could anything be more pitiful and mendacious? Her handkerchief was found in his bureau the night of the robbery. Where is the handkerchief now? He burned it! He found a note on a card from her hidden in the handkerchief she had given Hatton to replace in the drawer. Where is the card? He burned it! He 'purposely destroyed all evidence against her.' A sham Quixote! Who found her handkerchief in his bureau? Who saw the burning? Who put the handkerchief in the drawer?

Who told him of her confession? Who heard her beg that you should be delayed in your investigation? Who, in fact, is corroborating witness to everything and anything he alleges, but the man he believes, and I believe, you can never reach again. Hatton is failing rapidly."

"How could he have heard that?" asked Miller, with mingled wrath and stupefaction in his face,— wrath at the doctor's contemptuous disregard of all other opinions, and stupefaction at the suddenly presented view of the case.

"The attendant, sir, was down at the telegraph office when the news came in, and he had to tell McLean; the latter insisted on being told the truth. Weeks fears blood-poisoning, and if that has set in nothing can save him. Then where will be your evidence against this most foully wronged lady?"

"Hush!" exclaimed Miller, quickly, with a warning, sidelong glance toward Bedlam. "Come with me!" And, following his commander's look, the doctor saw, standing close together, leaning on the southern balustrade and gazing down upon them in evident interest and equally evident surprise, Fanny Forrest and Mr. Roswell Holmes. Silently he turned and accompanied the major until he reached his own gateway, and then stopped.

"I presume there is nothing further I can do just

now, and, with your permission, sir, I will leave you. I want to think this all over."

"Do so, doctor. And, when you are ready, come and see me. Let me only say this to you: You have hardly known McLean at all. We have known him nearly five years, and he has ever been in our eyes the soul of honor and truth."

"The soul of honor and truth, sir, would not be writing love-letters and destroying the peace of mind of a young and innocent girl when all he has to offer her is a millstone of debt and a tarnished name." And with this parting-shot the doctor majestically turned away.

"So that's where the shoe pinches!" thought Miller, as he entered his quarters, where presently he was joined by his excited wife.

"He isn't half as prostrated as you thought he'd be," she instantly exclaimed, as she entered the room. "Of course it wouldn't be Mac if he were not greatly distressed, but I have promised him that not a word shall leak out until Captain Forrest gets here, and that then he is to see him himself. Isn't it dreadful about Mr. Hatton? Can nothing be done?"

"I am to see Bayard again by and by. This affair has completely unstrung him, for he is evidently deeply smitten; I never dreamed it had gone so far. Now that letter must be written to the general, and

I am going to the office. You must not know a thing about it, or about this affair. Of course you will be besieged with questions." And so the major sallied forth.

Darkness was settling down. The sunset-gun had been fired just as they left McLean's. By this time the doctor should be entertaining his guest at dinner, and Miller wondered how even "Chesterfield" would rally to the occasion and preserve his suavity and courtliness after the shock of the last hour. But Miller had no idea that it was the last of three shocks that had assailed him in quick succession and with increasing severity that very day, and never dreamed of the gulf of distress in which poor Bayard was plunged. He had gone at once to his library and thrown himself in the easy-chair in an attitude of profound dejection, barely paying attention when Chloe entered to say that Miss Nellie begged to be excused from coming down to dinner, as she felt too ill. Then Robert entered to ask should he serve dinner or wait until Mr. Holmes came in. "Wait!" said Bayard, bluntly. But five minutes passed; the dinner would be overdone; so Robert slipped out in search of the truant, and Miller saw him going over to Bedlam. But the upper gallery was empty; Mr. Holmes and Miss Forrest had disappeared; the adjutant came striding up from the guard-house, and together the two officers turned away.

"Orderly," said the major, to the attendant soldier following at his heels, "find Sergeant Freeman, who is in charge of the cavalry detachment, and tell him I want him at once. Then go and get your supper."

Meantime, realizing that the dinner-hour was at hand, and knowing the punctilious ideas of his host, Mr. Holmes had somewhat abruptly bidden adieu to the young lady with whom he had been in such interesting conversation. "I must see you again about Hatton if possible, and just as soon as I have found out what this means. If all the four were together at McLean's room the mischief is probably done, but I'll see him at once unless it be forbidden." He was turning away without more words, when something in her deep, dark eyes seemed to detain him. He held forth his hand.

"Miss Forrest, I cannot tell you how I appreciate the honor you have done me in this confidence. It may be the means of my making more than one man happy. One word, where is Celestine now?"

"She should be in the dining-room, setting the table for tea. Good-by, then, till tattoo. See him if you can."

"Indeed I will," he answered, and bowing over the slender, richly-jewelled hand she so frankly placed in his, he slowly released it, and turned away.

"In the dining-room, is she?" muttered Holmes to

himself, as he ran lightly through the hall and down the stairs. "If that was not Miss Celestine I saw this moment scurrying in from the direction of the wood-piles out yonder, I'm vastly mistaken, and she was talking with a soldier there. I saw the glint of the sunset on the brasses of his forage-cap. I thought they all had to be at retreat roll-call, but this fellow missed it."

Turning at the foot of the stairs, he strode to the rear door, and looked out through the side-light upon the unpicturesqueness of the yards, the coal- and wood-sheds, the rough, unpainted board fences; the dismantled gate, propped in most inebriate style against its bark-covered post, and clinging thereto with but a single hinge. At this half-closed aperture suddenly appeared the mulatto girl, stopped, turned, gave a quick glance at the various back windows of Bedlam, waved her hand to a dim, soldierly form just discernible in the twilight striding toward the northern end of the garrison, then she came scurrying to the door, and burst in, panting.

"Ah, Celestine! That you?" asked Holmes, pleasantly. "I thought to find you in the dining-room, and stopped to ask for a glass of water."

At sight of him the girl had almost recoiled, but his cheery voice reassured her.

"Laws, Mr. Holmes! I done thought 'twas a

ghost," she laughed, but turned quickly from him as she spoke and hurried into the dining-room, filling a goblet with a trembling hand. He drank the water leisurely; thanked her, and strolled with his accustomed deliberation through the hall and out across the piazza, never appearing to notice her breathlessness or agitation. Once outside the steps, however, his deliberation was cast aside, and with rapid, nervous strides he hastened up the walk,—out past the old ordnance storehouse and the lighted windows of the trader's establishment, turned sharply to the west, and, sure enough, coming toward him was a brisk, dapper, slim-built little soldier in his snugly-fitting undress uniform. Holmes stopped short, whipped out his cigar-case and wind-matches, thrust a Partaga between his teeth, struck a light as the soldier passed him and the broad glare from the north window fell full upon the dapper shape and well-carried head. There was the natty forage-cap with the gleaming cross-sabres; there was the dark face, there the heavy brows, the glittering black eyes, the moustache and imperial, the close-curling hair, of the very man he had seen peeping into the parlor windows back of Mrs. Griffin's little post-office the night of his talk with Corporal Zook.

Ten minutes later and he was tapping at McLean's door. It was opened by the hospital attendant,—slowly and only a few inches.

"Can I see the lieutenant?" he asked.

"I am very sorry," whispered the man, mindful of the visitor's prodigality in the past and hopeful of future favors. "I have strict orders to admit nobody to-night until the doctor sees him again. The lieutenant isn't so well, sir, and Dr. Bayard had to administer sedatives before he left. I think he is sleeping just now, though he may only be trying to."

Holmes paused, reluctant and a little irresolute.

"Is there nothing I can do or say, sir, if he wakes?" asked the attendant.

"Can you give him a letter and say nothing about it to anybody?"

"Certainly I can,—if it's one that won't harm him."

"It will do him good, unless I'm mistaken; and he ought to have it to-night: he'll sleep better for it. I'll give it to you at tattoo.—Ah, Robert! I might have known you'd be in search of me and that I was delaying dinner. Say I'll be there instantly."

Meantime, Sergeant Freeman had reported to Major Miller as directed, and was standing attention, cap in hand, at that officer's desk, while the adjutant was scratching away across the room, his pen racing over the paper as he copied the despatch his commander had slowly and thoughtfully dictated.

"You say that Parsons is the best man to send, sergeant?"

"I don't say that, sir, exactly; but he's the lightest man in the troop and has the fastest horse now in the post. He could make it quicker than anybody else, but——"

"But what? Doesn't he want to go? Is he afraid?" asked the major, impatiently.

The sergeant flushed a little, as he promptly answered,—

"It isn't that, sir. He wants to go. There's no man in the troop, sir, that would be safe in saying he didn't want to go."

"Then why do you hesitate?"

"Because we don't know Parsons well, sir; he hasn't been with us more'n a year. He was Lieutenant Blunt's striker till the lieutenant was wounded, but Captain Terry had him returned to the troop because we were so short of men and had so much scouting to do. Then Parsons got into the office as company clerk, and that's where he is now, sir. He writes a fine hand and seemed to know all about papers."

"Where had he served before joining you?" asked the major.

"Nowhere, sir. He says he learned what he knows in the adjutant's office at St. Louis barracks, where they had the cavalry depot. He's been a barber, I think, on a Mississippi steamboat, but he can ride well."

"Well, let Parsons be the man. If he wants to go I see no reason why he shouldn't. Tell him to report here mounted and ready at tattoo."

But it was nearly ten o'clock before Parsons was ready,—a singular fact when it is remembered that he wanted to go,—and Mr. Holmes, who had stopped a moment to speak with Miss Forrest as the bugle ceased playing tattoo, found sufficient interest in their chat to detain him until just as the signal "Lights out" was ringing on the still night-air. Then a horse came trotting briskly into the garrison and over to the adjutant's office. Holmes caught a glimpse of the rider as he shot under the gallery and through the gleam from the lower windows. That face again!

Ten minutes afterward this inquisitive civilian was at the store, and, singling out one of half a dozen cowboys who were laughing and drinking at the bar, he beckoned him to come outside. The others followed, for the barkeeper, in obedience to post orders, was closing up his shop. Holmes led his silent follower beyond earshot of the loungers at the door-way.

"Did you see the soldier who rode past here just now?"

"Yes, sir."

"Drake, I've picked you out for service that I can intrust to no one else. You've never failed me yet. Are you ready for a long ride to-night?"

"Anything you want, Mr. Holmes."

"That man's orders are to go with all speed to Fetterman and, after resting there twenty-four hours, to take it easily returning. He'll go there all right, I believe, but what he does there and after he leaves there I want to know, if you have to follow to Cheyenne. Here's fifty dollars. If he jumps the track and starts for the railway after quitting Fetterman, let him go; wire me from Chugwater, but don't lose track of him. I'll join you at Cheyenne or Laramie City, wherever he goes, and the moment you strike the settlements put the sheriff on his trail."

XVIII.

THREE days slipped away without noticeable changes in the situation at Laramie. It was late on Tuesday evening when the courier rode away with his despatch, and on Wednesday afternoon the wire from Fetterman flashed the tidings of his safe arrival there and the prompt transmission of the packet in pursuit of the escort that had left for the north at morn. Miller breathed more freely, as did his good wife, as now the onus of this great source of distress would be shifted to other shoulders. "A family affair of much importance—no less than the more than probable connection of one of his household with a series of extensive thefts—demanded that Captain Forrest, if a possible thing, be sent hither at once," was the burden of the major's letter, and he knew that, if a possible thing, the general would find means of ordering the captain in on some duty which would give no inkling of the real nature of the ordeal awaiting him. Thursday afternoon, late, Parsons was to start on his return, would probably rest or camp at the deserted huts of the ranchmen at La Bonté, possibly at the "Lapperell," as the frontiersmen termed the little stream the French trappers had years before named

La Prêle, and should reach the fort some time Friday evening, though there was no hurry and he had full authority, if he saw fit, to rest his horse another night at Bull Bend or anywhere he pleased. No one in authority was giving that matter a thought, but it was exactly that matter that kept Roswell Holmes on the watch at Laramie when he would rather have gone away. To his keen eyes it was evident that, despite all Bayard's efforts to appear jovial and courteous as ever, he was in sore perplexity. Nellie, too, was again keeping her room, and Jeannie Bruce, with white face and red-rimmed eyes, was the only companion she really welcomed. Thursday night had come, and the letter he was to have handed in for McLean's benefit and peace of mind was still withheld. Any hour might enable him to speak positively, whereas now he could only theorize. Meantime, Mrs. Miller assured him that the young officer who " had been temporarily set back by the bad news from Mr. Hatton" was doing very well under the influence of better tidings. On Thursday morning a despatch from the stockade brought the welcome information from Dr. Weeks that Hatton's rugged constitution seemed proof against the enemy; he was gaining again.

Meantime, not a word did Miller, Bayard, or the adjutant breathe of that conference with McLean, and neither Mr. Holmes nor Miss Forrest could form the faintest idea of what had taken place. They had their theories and had frankly exchanged them, and what caused Mrs. Miller infinite amaze and the garrison a new excitement was this growing companionship between the Chicago millionaire and the "Queen of Bedlam." Thrice now had they been seen on the gallery *tête-à-tête*, and once, leaning on his arm, she had appeared on the walk. To the ladies there was no theory so popular as the one that she was setting her cap for him in good earnest now that Nellie Bayard was confined to her room; and when Mrs. Miller met him she longed to speak upon the subject. She could well-nigh thank any woman who could draw this formidable rival away and leave the ground to her wounded and deeply-smitten lieutenant; but could she see him becoming entangled in the toils of Miss Forrest, knowing what she did of that young woman's dreadful moral affliction? There was no way in which she could warn him. She had pledged her word to the major that not a whisper should escape, and though Mrs. Bruce had managed to derive from a conversation with her that Captain Forrest had been sent for, it was accomplished by that feminine device, now so successfully imitated by the so-called interviewers of the public press, of making assertions and hazarding suggestions which could not be truthfully denied. The lady longed to take Holmes into her confidence,—and could not; and Holmes longed to ask her what allegations had been made against McLean and how he had borne them,—yet dared not. Both to him and the Queen of Bedlam that was the explanation of the simultaneous gathering, at the quarters of the young officer, of the commandant, surgeon, and adjutant. Holmes boldly inquired of the doctor what had taken place, asserting that he was interested in McLean and wanted to help him, if he was in trouble; and in great embarrassment the doctor had begged to be excused from reply. He would not deny that McLean was in trouble,—in grave trouble,—but there was nothing tangible as yet. Nothing was to be said or done until —well, until he was much better and able to be about.

Friday afternoon came, warm, sunshiny, and delightful. At four o'clock the doctor's carriage—an open, easy, old-fashioned-looking affair—rolled out of the garrison with Nellie Bayard and Jeannie Bruce smiling on the back seat, while Bayard himself handled the reins. There was a vacant place beside him, and, just as he possibly expected, Miss Forrest came out on the gallery and waved her hand and smiled cordial greeting to the two girls. Instantly he reined in his eager horses, almost bringing them upon their haunches, and called up to her:

"This is the best piece of luck that has befallen me since I came to Laramie. I've caught you when you could not be engaged. Do come and join us, Miss Forrest! I'm taking my little invalid out for a drive in the sunshine, and it will do you, too, a world of good. Do come!"

But Miss Forrest's clear voice was heard in prompt and positive regret. It was impossible: she had an engagement that would occupy her a full hour, and while she thanked the doctor—thanked them all—for stopping for her, it could not be. "I am so glad to see you out again, Miss Nellie," she called. "Now, I shall hope to have you come and spend an hour with me over here."

The doctor could hardly conceal his chagrin. Again he begged. Again his offer was courteously but positively declined. Nellie gave but faint response to Miss Forrest's greetings. Jeannie Bruce looked fixedly away, and finally the horses received a sharp and most unnecessary touch of the lash, and went bounding away from "Bedlam" in a style that reflected small credit on the merits of the driver, and that nearly bruised the backs of his fair passengers.

Reclining half dressed, in a big easy-chair, Randall McLean heard the crash of the horses' hoofs and the whirr-r-r of the wheels on the gravelly road in front, and demanded of the attendant an account of the party.

"The doctor, sir, and the two young ladies—out for a drive."

McLean was silent for a moment. Mrs. Miller had gone home some time before on household cares intent, and the doctor was by this time out of the garrison. It left the patient master of the situation.

"Get this chair out on the gallery," he presently said, as he slowly raised himself to his feet and leaned for support against the table. "Put a robe and pillow in it. Then come back and help me out."

The soldier demurred and would have argued, but Mr. McLean silenced him, and presently, in his best blue fatigue-coat and with a white silk handkerchief around his neck and his fatigue-cap tilted over one eye, the young officer, leaning on the attendant's arm, slowly made his way into the open air and was soon comfortably ensconced in the big arm-chair again. Several men of his company, smoking on the piazza of the quarters across the parade, arose, put away their pipes, and came over to stand attention and salute their popular lieutenant, and to say how glad they were to see him able to sit up again. It touched McLean's sad and lonely heart to see the pleasure and the trust and faith in their brown, honest faces, and the tears came welling up to his eyes as he held out his hand, calling them by name to step up on the gallery where he could see them better and give each man a cordial though feeble response to the hearty pressure of their brawny hands. Then he bade the attendant, after a little chat about Mr. Hatton's condition and the more hopeful news, to take them in and give them a drink of Monongahela; but Corporal Stein promptly declined: he wouldn't have it thought they came with that hope, when their sole wish was to congratulate their young officer; and, though one or two of them, not so sensitive as the corporal, doubtless took him to task at a later moment, they one and all upheld him now. They would not go in and drink, but presently returned to their barracks, comforted with the reflection that they had done the proper thing.

Meantime, Miss Forrest had seen their approach, and, hearing the voices on the lower gallery, readily divined that Mr. McLean must be sitting up and taking the air. Five minutes after the men were gone, and as that young gentleman was wondering about what time the carriage would return, he heard a quick, light footstep along the wooden floor, the rustle of feminine skirts, and almost before he could turn, the cordial, musical voice of the Queen of Bedlam:

"Mr. McLean, how rejoiced I am to see you sitting up! This is simply delightful."

For an instant he knew not what to say—how to

greet her. Heavens! what thoughts of that gloomy council went surging through his brain. He tried to speak, tried to conceal his grievous embarrassment, but his gaunt face flushed painfully and the thin hand he extended in acknowledgment of hers was cold as ice. The nurse promptly brought a chair, set it close by the side of the big arm-chair; then as promptly vanished, as she gracefully thanked him and took it. This was a contingency that had not occurred to McLean for an instant. His whole idea had been to be where he could see Nellie's face, possibly receive a smile and bow, possibly a joyous word or two on her return. He had been able for the time being to forget all about Miss Forrest and the part he had been compelled to play in surrounding her with that web of evidence and suspicion, and now, at this most inopportune moment, here stood this gracious and graceful girl smiling at his side.

For a few moments more it was she who did most of the talking; Hatton, Captain Terry's Grays, and the fight down the Platte furnishing her with abundant material for blithe comment and congratulations. His constraint and solemnity of mien she attributed to physical suffering combined with distress of mind over the charges she believed to have been laid at his door; and, while avoiding all mention of that subject, it was her earnest desire to show him by every trick of woman's infinite variety and shade of manner that she had nothing but admiration for his soldierly conduct, and trust and friendship for him in his troubles. Poor Mac was but vague, unresponsive, and embarrassed in his acknowledgments, and then—she noted how his eyes were constantly wandering away up the road, and, with woman's quick intuition, divined that he was out there for no other purpose than to watch for the return of the doctor's carriage.

Presently it came in sight, driving rapidly, and, recalling everything that she had heard from Mr. Holmes in their recent talks of the doctor's distrust and antipathy toward McLean, Miss Forrest quickly arose and stepped to the end of the gallery. She had determined that the young soldier should not be balked in so modest a hope as that of seeing and being seen by the girl he loved. She felt assured that unless he was signalled or checked in some way the doctor would drive by "full tilt," and, with the quickness of thought, she had formed her plan. The sight of Fanny Forrest, standing at the north end of the gallery and holding aloft her white palm in the exact gesture of the Indian and frontiersman signalling "stop," was enough to make him bring the powerful team back on their haunches directly in front of the steps, and, before a word could be said in explanation, there, flushing feebly, was Randall McLean, striving to lift himself from his nest of robes and pillows, and salute the lady of his heart.

Lachlan stepped quickly forward from the hall and, with him on one side and Miss Forrest smiling on the other, McLean was half lifted to the railing, where he could look right into the bonnie face he longed to see. Nellie Bayard, sitting nearest him, flushed crimson at the first glimpse at the tall, gaunt figure, and her little hand tightly closed beneath the lap-robe on the sturdier fingers of Miss Bruce. A joyous light danced only one instant in her eyes, and died out as quickly as the flush upon her cheek at sight of Miss Forrest's supporting arm. Was this, then, the engagement which prevented her acceptance of the doctor's offer? Was this the way in which the hero of her girlish dreams should be restored to her,—with that bewilderingly handsome and fascinating New York girl at his side, almost possessively supporting and exhibiting him? The sight had stung the doctor too, and the same idea about the engagement seemed .to flash through his head.

"This will never do, Mr. McLean," he sternly spoke, "you are in no condition to venture out; I'll be over to see you in a minute. Get back to your room as quick as you can." And with these words he whipped up his team again, and the carriage flashed away. Nellie had not spoken a word.

For a moment they stood there stunned. McLean gazed bitterly after the retreating vehicle a moment, then turned with questioning eyes to his silent companion. She, too, was gazing fixedly after the doctor's little party, her color fluttering, her eyes glowing, and her white teeth setting firmly. Then impulsively she turned to him:

"This is all my fault, all my stupidity, Mr. McLean; I might have known. Forgive me for the sake of my good intentions, and depend upon it, good shall yet come of this, for now I have a crow to pick with Dr. Bayard, and I mean to see him before he sees you. Are you going in,—at once?"

"Yes. There's nothing else to do," he answered, wearily, hopelessly, wretchedly, as he slowly turned away.

"Mr. McLean!" she exclaimed, with sudden and irrepressible excitement of manner. "Stop!—one moment only. There's something I must say to you. Lachlan, please step inside the hall," she hurriedly continued. "I'll call you in plenty of time before the doctor can get here. Now, Mr. McLean, listen! I know something of your trouble. I know something of the toils by which you have been surrounded, and how unjustly you have been treated; but let me tell you that the very man you have most feared is the man of all others who stands your steadfast friend. Look! He's coming now. Coming fast, too—from the telegraph office. I almost know what it is he brings. One more thing I must say while yet there is time. I could not help seeing how your heart was bound up in Nellie Bayard. Nay, don't turn away in such despair. I read her better than you do, and I know you better than you think. I tell you brighter days are near. Keep up a brave heart, Mr. McLean. Remember your name; remember 'The race of Clan Gillian—the fearless and free.' I tell you that were I a man I could envy you the truth I read in Nellie Bayard's eyes. All is coming out well, and there's my hand and my heart full of good wishes with it."

He took it wonderingly, silently. Good heavens! Was this the woman who, through his testimony, stood accused of degrading crimes? Was it possible that she could have been the criminal, and yet at the very time could write those mysterious words upon the hidden card—proffering aid and friendship? What manner of woman was this now quivering with excitement at his side, her glowing eyes fastened on the rapidly advancing form of Roswell Holmes? What meant she by speaking of the man he most feared as his most steadfast friend?

Just as Major and Mrs. Miller with Dr. Bayard

stepped upon the broad gallery of Bedlam at its southern end and stopped in embarrassment at sight of the group at the other, Mr. Holmes had bounded up the steps and, placing in her hand a telegraphic despatch, held forth his own to Randall McLean.

"Read it aloud!" was all he said, and eagerly she obeyed:

"CHUGWATER, Friday, 4 P.M.

"ROSWELL HOLMES, ESQ., Fort Laramie.—Parsons streaking it for Cheyenne. Has plenty money. Close at his heels.

"DRAKE."

XIX.

WHATEVER sensation or suppressed mystery may have existed at the post prior to the receipt of the brief despatch announcing that the soldier, Parsons, had "bolted," it was all as nothing compared with the excitements of the week that followed. Miller's first impulse, when Mr. Holmes placed the brown scrap of paper in his hands, was to inquire how it happened that a civilian should concern himself with the movements of his men, either in or out of garrison, but something in the expression of Miss Forrest's face as she walked calmly past him on the way to her room, and in the kindling eyes of this popular and respected gentleman gave him decided pause.

"There is a matter behind all this which I ought to know, is there not?" was therefore his quiet inquiry; and when Mr. Holmes assured him that there was, and the two went off together arm in arm, leaving Mrs. Miller to wonder what it all could mean, and to go in and upbraid her pet lieutenant for venturing from his room when still so weak, it was soon evident to more eyes than those of Dr. Bayard that something of unusual interest was indeed brewing, and that the ordinarily genial and jovial major was powerfully moved. In ten minutes the two men were at the telegraph office and the operator was "calling" Cheyenne. An hour later, after another brief and earnest talk with Miss Forrest on the upper gallery of "Bedlam," Mr. Holmes's travelling wagon rolled into the garrison and away he went. At midnight he was changing horses at "The Chug." The next day he was at Cheyenne and wired the major from that point. Two days more and he was heard from at Denver, and then there was silence.

At the end of the week Private Parsons, of Terry's Grays, who had been carried for three or four successive mornings as "on detached service," then as "absent without leave," was formally accounted for as "deserted," and it began to be whispered about the garrison that grave and decidedly sensational reasons attended his sudden disappearance. Dr. Bayard had a long and private interview with the commanding officer, who showed him a letter received from Mr. Holmes, and went home to Nellie with a dazed look on his distinguished face. The sight of Randall McLean, seated on the front piazza, and in blithe conversation with that young lady and her friend Miss Bruce, for an instant caused him to halt short at his own gate, but, mastering whatever emotion possessed him, the doctor marched straight up to that rapidly recuperating officer, who was trying to find his feet and show due respect to the master of the house, and, bidding him keep his seat, bent over and took his hand and confused him more than a little by the unexpected and really inexplicable warmth of his greeting.

McLean, who had been accustomed to constraint and coldness of manner on the part of the post surgeon, was at a loss to account for the sudden change. Nellie, whose sweet eyes had marked with no little uneasiness her father's hurried coming, flushed with relief and shy delight at this unlooked-for welcome; and Jeannie Bruce, to use her own expression when telling of it afterward, was "all taken aback." She and Mrs. Miller had between them planned that Mr. McLean should walk over with the latter, early in the afternoon, just as though out for a little airing and to try his legs after their unaccustomed rest. Nellie and Miss Bruce were to happen out on the piazza at the moment (and the details of this portion of the plan were left to the ingenuity of "Bonnie Jean" herself, who well knew that it must be accomplished without a germ of suspicion on the part of her shy and sensitive little friend), and McLean was to be escorted in by Mrs. Miller, who was presently to leave, promising to come back for him in a few moments. Then, when the ice was broken and Nellie was beginning to feel more at ease after the mysterious estrangement and this sudden reappearance of her old friend, Jean, too, was to be called away and the pair be left alone. Arch plotters that these women are! They had chosen the hour when the doctor almost invariably took his siesta, and both ladies had warned their friends on no account to select that opportunity to rush over and congratulate the lieutenant on his convalescence,—a thing the Gordon girls would have been sure to do. Miss Bruce had gone so far as to ask Mrs. Miller if she did not think it might be well to "post" Miss Forrest, who had been almost daily seen conversing with Mr. McLean since he began to sit out on the gallery again; but Mrs. Miller promptly replied that there was no need to tell Miss Forrest anything. "She has more sense than all of the rest of us put together," were the surprising words of the reply, "as I have excellent reasons to know."

What could have happened to so radically change Mrs. Miller's estimate of and regard for the "Queen of Bedlam?" was Jean Bruce's natural question of her mother that night, and Mrs. Bruce was in a quandary how to answer and not betray the secret that had been confided to her. From having avoided and distrusted Miss Fanny Forrest, it was now noticeable to the entire garrison that Mrs. Miller was exerting herself to be more than civil.

It was too late to change the plan of the afternoon's campaign when the major's orderly came around to Dr. Bayard's with the compliments of the commanding officer and a request that the doctor join him at his quarters as soon as possible. Although he was gone nearly an hour, he returned before McLean had been with the girls more than a quarter of that time, and changed their apprehension into wonderment and secret joy by the extreme—almost oppressive—courtesy of manner to his unbidden guest.

"It was just as though he was trying to make amends for something," said Miss Bruce, in telling of it afterward. Be that as it may, it is certain that after urging McLean to take a good rest where he was and to come again, and "sun himself" on their piazza, and being unaccountably cordial in his monologue (for the younger officer hardly knew how to express himself under the circumstances), the doctor finally vanished. Jeannie Bruce was so utterly "taken aback" by it all that for some minutes she totally forgot her part in the little drama. Then, suddenly recalling the rôle she was to play, despite the appeal and protest and dismay in Elinor's pleading eyes, Miss Bruce, too, sped away and the two were left alone. From the south end of the gallery at Bedlam Miss Forrest looked smilingly upon the scene and would fain have rewarded Bonnie Jean by blowing a kiss to her, but Jeannie's eyes were focussed on a little party of horsemen just dismounting in front of the commanding officer's. They might bring news from the cantonment,—perhaps a little note from her own particular hero, Mr. Hatton.

Nearing them she recognized the leader as a sergeant of Captain Terry's troop, and knew well from the trim appearance of the men and their smooth-shaven cheeks and chins that they were just setting forth, not just returning from the field. The adjutant came hurrying down the steps of the major's quarters just as she reached the gate, and raised his forage-cap at sight of her.

"You can start at once, sergeant," she heard him say. "Now remember: to-morrow evening will be time enough for you to land your party at Fort Russell. Report on arrival to the commanding officer, and permit none of your men to go into Cheyenne until he sends you. Then you are to return here with whatever may be intrusted to your care."

She was not at all surprised on reaching home to find her mother and Mrs. Miller watching with eager eyes the departure of the cavalrymen. McLean and Nellie Bayard saw it too, and it gave them something to talk about a whole hour that afternoon, and paved the way for another talk the next day—and the next.

That night, in quick succession, the telegraph brought four despatches to Laramie. As in duty bound, the messenger went first to the commanding officer, who held out his hand for all four and was surprised at being accorded only two. "These are for Miss Forrest, sir," said the messenger. The major broke the envelope of his own, glanced at the first, and snapped his fingers with delight and exultation.

"They've got him, Lizzie!" he chuckled to his eager helpmate. Then he tore open the other. The glad look vanished in an instant; the light of hope, relief, and satisfaction fled from his eyes and the color from his cheeks. "My God!" he muttered, as his hand fell by his side.

"What is it, dear?" she queried, anxiously.

"Forrest is coming—post-haste. Will be here to-morrow night. Now she's got to be told."

"Then, as it is all my fault, I must be the one," was the reply.

But even as they were discussing the matter, irresolute, distressed, there was a ring at the bell; and in a moment who should enter the parlor, holding in her hand those fateful telegrams, but Miss Forrest herself? She came straight toward them—smiling, and Mrs. Miller and her half-dazed major arose to greet her.

"I suppose I may be taken into official confidences to-night; may I not, major?" she said, gayly. "Mr. Holmes has probably wired us news which we can exchange. I congratulate you on the recovery of your deserter, and you can rejoice with me in the recovery of my diamonds."

"Your diamonds!" exclaimed the major and his good wife in a breath. "When—how were they taken? Why did you not tell us?"

"They were taken from my room—from my locked trunk—the night of Dr. Bayard's dinner,—the same night that his porte-monnaie and his beautiful amethyst set were stolen from Mr. Holmes. I did not tell any one at first, because of Mrs. Forrest's prostrated condition, and because at first I suspected her servant Celestine and thought I could force her into restoring them without letting poor Ruth know anything about it. Then I couldn't speak of it, for the next discovery I made simply stunned me and made me ill. Then, finally, I told Mr. Holmes, and he took the matter in charge. You have heard from my brother, too?" she asked eagerly. "I am rejoiced at his coming, for it will do her a world of good, and she is wild with excitement and happiness now. How was it all managed, major? He wrote to me a fortnight ago that with the prospect of incessant fighting before them it was impossible for him to ask for leave of absence, and begging me to help Ruth in every way in my power and save her from worry of any kind. You see how I was placed. And now, all of a sudden, he is virtually ordered in, he wires me, and can attribute it to nothing but dangerous illness on her part. Did you get it for him? I *know* you did."

Miller and his wife looked at her, then at one another in dumb amaze. What could he say? How could he force himself to tell this brave and spirited and self-sacrificing girl of the cloud of suspicion with which she had been enveloped!

"Tell me about the diamonds," gasped Mrs. Miller to gain time. "Were they valuable? Though of course they must have been. Everything of yours is so beautiful and—well, I must say it all now—costly."

"They were a present from my uncle, Mr. Courtlandt," she answered, simply. "I valued them more than anything I had. The trunk was entered by false keys, and the diamonds were taken out of their locked case and spirited away. My first suspicion attached to Celestine and her soldier friend. They had been aroused before at Robinson. Then came this stunning surprise in my discovery next day, and a week of great indecision and distress. Now, of course, the inspiration of the villany is captured, though more than ever do I suspect Celestine as being confederate, or possibly principal actor. She has been utterly daft the last four days and constantly haunting the post-office for a letter that never comes."

"She will be wild enough when she knows the truth," said Miller, hoarsely. "The scoundrel had a wife in Denver, where he was finally tracked and jailed. It was she who offered the diamonds in pawn. They did not manage things well, and should have waited, for he had over two hundred dollars,—must have had,—for you and Mr. Holmes were not the only losers here."

"Who were the others?" she quickly asked.

"Mr. Hatton and Mr. McLean."

"Mr. McLean! Oh, the shame of it!" Miss Forrest paced rapidly up and down the parlor floor, her eyes flashing, her cheeks flushed, her hands nervously twisting the filmy handkerchief she carried. Her excitement was something utterly foreign to her, and neither Miller nor his wife could understand it. Suddenly, as though by uncontrollable impulse, she stopped before and faced them.

"Major Miller!" she exclaimed, "I must tell you something. I had made up my mind to do it yesterday. It will not add to my faint popularity here, but I respect you and Mrs. Miller. I know you are *his* friends, and I want your advice. How am I to make amends to Mr. McLean? What am I to say to him? Do you know that for a few days of idiocy I was made to believe that you suspected him of the thefts? and it was his handkerchief I found on the floor behind my trunk. What will the man think of me? And yet I *must* tell him. I cannot sit by him day after day, see him, speak with him, and have my heart hammering out the words, 'He thinks you are his friend, and you thought him to be a thief.'"

It was more than Miller could stand. "Miss Forrest! Miss Forrest!" he exclaimed, as his wife sank into an easy-chair and hid her face in her hands. "You cover me with shame and confusion. Never in my life have I heard of so extraordinary a complication as this has been! never have I been so worried and distressed! My dear young lady, try and hear me patiently. You have been far more sinned against than sinning. A few hours ago Dr. Bayard—he who led you in your suspicions, for he told me so—left here crushed and humbled to find that he had been so blind and unjust. But I would gladly exchange places with him, for I've been worse. I've been weak enough to be made to look with other's eyes and not my own. McLean was indeed involved in grave suspicion, but nothing as compared with that which surrounded another,—a woman who was entitled to our utmost sympathy and protection because her natural protector was in the field far from her side,—a woman who did find friends and protectors in my young officers,—McLean and Hatton,—God bless 'em for it! for they stoutly refused to tell a thing until it was dragged from them by official inquiry, and then they had burned every tangible piece of evidence against her. She was at Robinson last winter, and money and valuables were constantly disappearing. Silken skirts were heard trailing in dark hall-ways at night; her form was seen in the room of the plundered officers. The stories followed her to Laramie. The night McLean and Hatton were robbed her silken skirts were heard trailing up the north hall of Bedlam and her feet scurrying over the gallery. Her handkerchief was found at McLean's bureau, and, while they were all waiting for her at Mrs. Gordon's, McLean himself collided with a feminine shape in the darkness out on the parade, and it slipped away without a word as though fearing detection. The night of the robbery at Bayard's she was alone up-stairs. Another night she was seen entering the hall-way without ringing the bell or knocking at the door. Another evening I, who was in the Bayards' library, listened for ten minutes to some one who was striving to pick the lock and make a secret entrance while Elinor was confined to her room and the doctor was known to be a quarter of a mile away at the hospital. At last, wearying of waiting for the thief to effect an entrance and permit of my seeing him or her in the hall, I sprang out upon the piazza and found—you. Then that night I strove to see Hatton and wring from him his knowledge of what had been going on in Bedlam. You implored him not to go. You, unwittingly, made him and, through him, McLean believe it was your own trouble you sought to conceal; and, though I thank God I was utterly mistaken, utterly wrong in my belief, I crave your forgiveness, Miss Forrest. It was I who urged that your brother be sent here at once, though the general believes it was on Mrs. Forrest's account, that he might put an end to these peculations and restore what property could be recovered from you,—you who have suffered a loss far greater than all the others put together and never said a word about it."

And poor Miller, who had never made so long a speech in his life before, turned chokingly away. Then Mrs. Miller spoke, and Miss Forrest's dilated eyes were turned slowly from the major's bulky shape to the matronly form upon the sofa and the woe-begone face that appeared from behind the handkerchief. Miss Forrest's cheeks had paled and her lips were parted. She had seized and was leaning upon the back of a chair, but not one word had she spoken. As Mrs. Miller's voice was heard, it seemed as though a slight contraction of the muscles brought about a decided frown upon her white forehead, but she listened in utter silence.

"Indeed, Miss Forrest, you musn't blame the major too much. He wouldn't have listened to a word against you—if—if it hadn't been for me. I was all at fault. But I couldn't have believed a word against you had it not been for those letters from Robinson. They—they——"

And here Mrs. Miller had recourse to her handkerchief, and Miss Forrest stretched forth her hand as though to urge her say no more. There was intense silence in the parlor a moment. Then through the open windows came the sudden sound of a scuffle, a woman's shriek, a sudden fall, voluble curses and ravings in Celestine's familiar tones, and the rush of many feet toward Bedlam.

Seizing his cap and hurrying thither, the major pushed his way through an excited group on the lower gallery. The sergeant of the guard, lantern in hand, was wonderingly contemplating the Scotch "striker" Lachlan, who firmly clung to the wrist of the struggling, swearing girl, despite her adjurations to let her go. Other men from the quarters were clustered around them, hardly knowing what to say; for Lachlan contented himself with the single word "thief!" and never relaxed his grasp until the major bade him do so, but instantly renewed it as his prisoner attempted to spring away. McLean came limping to the scene from the direction of the doctor's quarters just as Miss Forrest, too, appeared, and him Lachlan addressed:

"I found her rummaging in the bureau, sir."

And then Miss Forrest's quiet voice was heard as soon as the major's orders to bring a gag had silenced the loud protestations and accusations of the negress.

"It is as we supposed, major. That is the skirt of an old silk I gave her last winter."

An hour later Celestine was locked in a room at the laundress's quarters, where stout "Mrs. Sergeant Flynn" organized an Amazon guard of heroines, who, like herself, had followed the drum for many a year; who assured the major the prisoner would never escape from their clutches, and whose motto appeared to be, "Put none but Irishwomen on guard to-night."

XX.

CONFESSIONS, of various sorts, were the order of the day at Laramie during the week that followed this important arrest, and then the fortnight of accusation was at an end. Parsons, the deserter, led off the day after his return to the post under escort of the little squad sent down from Terry's troop to meet him at Cheyenne. He was stubborn and silent at first, but when told by the corporal of the guard that Celestine had "gone back on him the moment she heard he had a wife at Denver, and had more than given him away," he concluded that it was time to deny some of the accusations heaped upon his head by the furious victim of his wiles. The girl had indeed obeyed his beck and will, and shielded him even in the days of suspense that followed his desertion; but no word can describe the rage of her jealousy, the fury of her hate, the recklessness of her tongue when she found that he had used her only as a tool to enrich another woman,—his lawful wife. Parsons told his story to an interested audience as though he had rather enjoyed the celebrity he had acquired, and Major Miller, Dr. Bayard, Captain Forrest, and Mr. Roswell Holmes were his most attentive listeners. He had been a corporal in the Marine Corps at the Washington Navy-Yard, and had seen Dr. Bayard many a time. Reduced to the ranks for some offence, he had become an officer's servant, and was employed at the mess-room, where Bayard must have seen him frequently, as the doctor rarely missed their festivities at the barracks. Here his peculations began and were discovered. He deserted and got to St. Louis, where he began to "barber" on a boat; got married and into more trouble; fled to Denver and found people's wits too sharp for him; so, leaving his wife to support herself as best she could, he ran up to Cheyenne and enlisted in the cavalry. Doors and windows, desks and trunks, were found lying open everywhere at Robinson; Celestine was speedily induced to learn the business, and proved an adept. He warned her she would be suspected, but she laughed and said she knew how to hoodwink folks. They kept up their partnership at Laramie, he receiving and hiding the valuables she brought him; but he was sure the doctor had recognized him; he knew there was danger, and he was determined to slip away the first chance that came, especially after securing the diamonds. The Fetterman despatch gave him the longed-for opportunity. Celestine was quieted by the promise that, as soon as the thing had blown over and he was safe, he would get word to her where to join him, send her plenty of money, and then they would be married and live happily ever after. On the way back from Fetterman he stopped at an abandoned hut near Bull Bend, where he had hidden his plunder on the way up, stowed the money and jewels in his saddle-bags, then pushed for Hunton's on the Chug; got safely by in the night, rode his horse hard to Lodge Pole Creek, where he left him at a ranch and secured the loan of another. Then keeping well to the west of Fort Russell and never going near Cheyenne, he crossed the Union Pacific and made his way to Denver. But there, to his dismay, the "Rocky Mountain" detective officials were on the watch for him, and every precaution had been vain. He was captured; Miss Forrest's diamonds, Mr. Holmes's amethysts, and Mr. Hatton's pins were found secreted in his possession, though most of the money was gone,—gambling,—and that was all. He never knew that Mr. Holmes had tracked him all the way and rolled up a volume of evidence against him.

Celestine, tiger-cat that she was, had at first filled the air with shrieks of rage and loud accusations, first against Lachlan and then Miss Forrest, but the Irish laundresses only jeered at her; and, when the deserter was fairly back in the garrison and the circumstances of his capture were made known, taunted her with having been victimized by a man who had a wife to share the profits of her plundering. Once made to realize that this was truth, she no longer sought to conceal anything. She seemed bent only on heaping up vengeance upon him. 'Twas he who corrupted her; he who taught her to steal; he who showed her how to pick locks; he who told her to wear Miss Forrest's silk skirts and steal her handkerchiefs and leave them where they would be found; he who let her in to the doctor's the night of the dinner and stole the portemonnaie from the fur coat while she went up-stairs and took the amethysts from Mr. Holmes's room. She wasn't afraid. If any one came all she had to do was to say she had returned for something she had lost when accompanying Miss Forrest. 'Twas he who told her to take some of McLean's handkerchiefs and drop one in Mr. Holmes's room where he would be sure to get it, "'cause Dr. Bayard wanted to get rid of Mr. McLean and would believe nothing against Miss Forrest;" 'twas he who tried to pick that latch again and get in and steal the doctor's silver, but was interrupted by Miss Forrest's coming, and had just time to slink away on tiptoe around the corner of the house; 'twas he who gave her keys to open Miss Forrest's trunk and showed her how to pick the lock of the little box that held her diamonds, and he who bade her lose one of McLean's handkerchiefs behind the trunk. Oh, yes! She was ready to swear fire, murder, and treason against him—her scoundrelly deceiver. In one short day this precious pair had succeeded in saddling each other with the iniquities of the garrison for a month back, and all other suspicions were at an end.

But there was still another feather in Mr. Holmes's cap. He had known these Denver detectives for years and had placed much valuable business in their hands. He had munificently rewarded every man who had been efficient in the present chase and capture; had had the pleasure of restoring to Miss Forrest in a new case and well-repaired setting the diamonds of which she had been despoiled, and then he sought McLean.

"Did you ever get a little card I left in your drawer one night while I was here with Mr. Hatton?" he asked.

McLean looked up in eager interest. "A card?— yes, but never dreamed it was from you. Indeed I thought—I was told—it came from an entirely different source, and it has puzzled me more than words can tell you."

"It was perhaps a piece of officiousness on my part, but we were in a peculiar state just then with all these thefts going on. I stowed it in one of your handkerchiefs while Hatton was out. What did you do with it?"

"Burned it—long ago. I couldn't understand at

all. It said that one who had been as hard pressed as I was—pecuniarily, I supposed—wanted to be my friend, and——"

"Yes, that's about it! I suppose you couldn't see your way clear to accepting help from me——"

"I didn't know it was your card or your writing. No initials appeared. The card was otherwise blank, and Hatton and I—well—there's no sense in telling the absurdity of our beliefs at that time. We were all at sea."

"Let all that pass," said Holmes, with a grave smile on his face. "The man that hasn't been a fool in one way or another in this garrison during the last month or so is not on my list of acquaintances, and I think I know myself. What I want now is a description of Sergeant Marsland. One of my Denver friends thinks he has spotted him as a swell gambler down at El Paso."

And so, that night, a full pen-picture of the lamented commissary-sergeant was wired to Denver. Two days later a special detective was speeding southward; and though Roswell Holmes had left Fort Laramie and gone about his other affairs long before the result was known, and long before the slow-moving wheels of Wyoming and military justice had rolled the two later culprits before the courts, it was his name that came up for renewed applause and enthusiastic praise when the telegraph brought to the commanding officer the news that a "rich haul!" had been made on the far-away Texan frontier. Marsland and over one thousand dollars had been gathered in at "one fell swoop."

Then came July, its blazing sunshine tempered by the snow-cooled breezes from the mountain-peaks, and its starry nights made drowsy and soothing by the softer melody of the swift-rushing Laramie. The roar and fury of the May torrents were gone and with them the clouds and storms of human jealousies and suspicions. The crowded garrison had undergone a valuable experience. The social circle of the post had learned a lesson as to the fallibility of feminine and masculine—judgment. Bruce was slyly ridiculing Miller because of his surrender to the views and theories of his better half, and, even while resenting verbally the fact that he had been excluded from all participation in the momentous affairs of the early summer, was known to be devoutly thankful in his innermost heart that he had not been drawn into the snarl. Bruce was hand in glove with Captain Forrest now, who, having set his house in order and silenced the querulous complaints of his wife at the loss of Celestine, was eager to get back to his troop. Between Forrest and McLean, too, there had sprung up a feeling of cordial friendship. Forrest had heard from his sister's lips the story of how he and Hatton had burned her handkerchief and striven in every way to shield her in his absence, and the cavalryman's heart warmed to them more than he could express. To Miller and McLean he told the story of his sister's differences with her uncle, pretty much in effect as Mrs. Forrest told the doctor. It was Courtlandt's son she would not marry because of his repeated lapses into inebriety, and Courtlandt's bounty she would no longer accept since she could not take the son. The registered letters she had mailed contained the remittances the sorrowful old man persisted in sending her and she persisted in returning. Dr. Bayard, too, had shown vast cordiality to the stalwart cavalry brother, but Forrest seemed to share his sister's views, and only moderately responded.

Poor Bayard! Again and again did he curse the cruel fates that had exiled him to this outlying, barbarous, incomprehensible community. Again and again did he bemoan the blunders he had made. In the *éclaircissement* that followed the arrest of Celestine and Parsons he had striven to pose as the champion of Miss Forrest and to redouble his devotions. There was no doubt of his devotion : the grandiose old beau was completely fascinated by the brilliancy, daring, and self-control of that indomitable Queen of Bedlam. After the first shock and a few hours of solitude, in which she refused to see or talk with anybody, Miss Forrest had emerged from her room in readiness to welcome her brother on his arrival, and no one in all that garrison could detect the faintest sign of resentment or discomposure in her manner. If anything, she was rather more approachable to people she could not fancy than at any time before, and, now that the Bruces and Gordons and Johnsons and everybody seemed in mad competition to see who could be most cordial and friendly with her, it speedily became apparent that it was their offishness, not hers, that had kept them asunder earlier in her visit. Mrs. Post had found her out, she proudly asserted, just as soon as she came to live under the same roof with her, and it was now her privilege to claim precedence over the others of the large sisterhood. But all this sudden popularity of the young lady in question was no great comfort to Bayard, who found it almost impossible to see her alone. She would gladly have gone to spend hours with Elinor, who was still far from strong, for "her Majesty," as she was often playfully referred to, was disposed to be very fond of that sweet-faced child; but Elinor seemed to shrink from her a little. She feared that her father had really fallen deeply in love again, and if so who could resist him? She admired Miss Forrest and could be very fond of her, but not as a second mother. Another matter that stood in the way of going thither was the fact that Bayard seemed to track her everywhere, and the situation was becoming unendurable. One night, at last, he dropped in at the Millers' when she was there, and promptly, when she retired, offered to escort her home. She thanked him, took his arm, walked slowly with him to the south hall of Bedlam, and there bid him adieu. No one knows just what was talked of on that eventful walk, but it was the last he ever sought with her, and for weeks Bayard was a moody, miserable man. All Laramie swore he had proposed and had been rejected, but no one could positively tell.

Elinor redoubled her loving ways from that time, and strove to cheer and gladden him, but he was almost repellent. There was only one thing, he declared to her, that made him wretched, and that was her attachment to Mr. McLean. If she would only be sensible, and see how absurd that was, he could smile again, but that was a matter in which his little girl had decided as her mother had decided before her. Poor Bayard! To revenge himself on his father- and mother-in-law he had wrested this sweet child from their arms and brought her hither, only to see her won away in turn, and, by all that was horrible, by an army lieutenant. He had to admit that McLean was a gentleman, a splendid officer, without a vice or a meanness, and, now that the stolen stores were replaced by their money value, without a debt in the world; but he was poor,—he was nothing, in fact, but what he himself had been when he won Elinor's mother. McLean had spoken to him manfully and asked his consent, but he rebuffed him, saying she was a mere child. McLean declared he would wait any reasonable time, but claimed the privilege of visiting her as a suitor, and this he would have refused, and for a few days did refuse, until her pallor and tearful eyes so upbraided him that he gave up in despair. Meantime she had poured out her heart to the loving grandparents at home, and they took her part, and, almost to her surprise, actually welcomed the news that she had a lover. The judge wrote to Bayard (the first time he had so honored him since their difference the previous winter), saying he knew "the stock" well and expressing his hearty approval of Nellie's choice. As to her future, he said, that was his business. It made no difference to him whether Mr. McLean was rich or poor. That matter was one he could settle to suit himself. It was a comfort to know she "had given her heart to a steadfast, loyal, and honest man." And so, having stirred up his son-in-law and made him wince to his heart's content, the old statesman bade him stand no longer in the way, but tell the young gentleman that he, too, would be glad to know him; and this letter, that evening, "old

Chesterfield" placed in his daughter's hand and then magnanimously gave her his blessing. It was not to be shown to McLean, said the doctor, but he did not tell her why. He was afraid the young fellow would read between the lines and see what the judge was driving at when he spoke of the loyalty and honesty of Nellie's lover.

Heavens! What billing and cooing there was at Laramie all that late summer and autumn! How Jeannie Bruce blushed and bloomed when the ambulance finally landed Mr. Hatton at her side, and he took his limping but blissful daily walk in her society! How Nellie Bayard's soft cheeks grew rounder and rosier as the autumn wore away, and how her sweet eyes softened and glowed as they gazed up into the manly face of the young soldier whom she was just beginning to learn (very shyly and hesitatingly yet, and only when none but he could hear) to call "Randall." Rapturous confidences were those in which she and Jeannie Bruce daily engaged. Blissful were the glances with which they rewarded Miss Forrest for her warm and cordial congratulations. Delightful were the hours they presently began to spend with her; and dismal, dismal was the old frontier post when October came and those three young women with appropriate escort were spirited away together: Elinor to spend the winter with her grandparents and make who knows what elaborate preparations for the military wedding which was to come off in the following May; Jeannie Bruce to pay her a long visit and indulge in similar, though far less lavish, shopping on her own account; and Miss Forrest to return to the roof of old Mr. Courtlandt, who begged it as a solace to his declining years and fast-failing health. The doctor, McLean, and Hatton went with the party as far as Cheyenne and saw them, with their friends Major and Mrs. Stannard, of the cavalry, safely aboard the train for Omaha, and then with solemn visages returned to the desolation of their post to worry through the winter as best they could. Telegrams from Omaha and Chicago told of the safe and happy flight of the eastward travellers, and soon the letters began to come. "What do you think?" wrote both the younger girls, "who do you suppose was at Chicago to meet us but Mr. Holmes?"

"All's well that ends well!" quoth Mr. Hatton, one evening soon after, as he blew a cloud of "Lynchburg sun-cured" tobacco-smoke across the top of the old Argand and tossed McLean a Cheyenne paper. "Celestine has gone to the penitentiary, and here's the sentence of the court in the case of Marsland and Parsons,—five years apiece." "All's well that ends well!" for those were glad and hopeful and happy hearts, as the long, long winter wore away and another May-day came around; and the sunshine danced on the snow crests of the grand old peak; and the foaming Laramie again tossed high its brawling surges; and the south wind swept away the few remaining drifts, searching them out in the depths of the bare ravines and bringing to light tender little tufts of green—the baby buffalo-grass: and one day there came a wild surprise, and the ladies swarmed to Mrs. Miller's for confirmation of the news that went from lip to lip,—the news that "her Majesty" had indeed at last surrendered, and that Roswell Holmes had wooed and won "The Queen of Bedlam."

THE END.

A LIST OF BOOKS

SELECTED FROM THE

Catalogue

—OF—

J. B. LIPPINCOTT COMPANY.

(COMPLETE CATALOGUE SENT ON APPLICATION.)

ENTERTAINING STORIES.
By FRANCES COURTENAY BAYLOR.

ON BOTH SIDES.

Containing "The Perfect Treasure" and "On This Side," the whole forming a complete story.

12mo. Extra Cloth. $1.25.

"No such faithful, candid, kindly, brilliant, and incisive presentation of English and American types has before been achieved. The wit of the story is considerable. It is written brilliantly, yet not flimsily. It is the best international novel that either side has hitherto produced. It is written by an American woman who really knows both countries, and who has shown that she possesses powers which ought to put her in the front rank of fiction."—*New York Tribune.*

BEHIND THE BLUE RIDGE.
A HOMELY NARRATIVE.

12mo. Extra Cloth. $1.25.

"Intensely dramatic in construction, rich in color, picturesque in description, and artistic in its setting."—*Philadelphia Record.*

"It is lightened through and through by humor as subtle and spontaneous as any that ever brightened the dark pages of life history, and is warmed by that keen sympathy and love for human nature which transfigures and ennobles everything it touches."—*Chicago Tribune.*

A SHOCKING EXAMPLE,
AND OTHER SKETCHES.

12mo. Extra Cloth. $1.25.

No stories of recent date are so tender and sympathetic; so rich in color; so bubbling over with humor, and so full of delicate etchings of pleasant life as those told by Miss Baylor. The present book embraces no less than fifteen complete sketches which are characterized by the same brilliancy of style that has won for the author's previous works the highest encomiums of the press and her large number of readers.

⁎ For sale by all Booksellers, or will be sent by the Publishers, postpaid, on receipt of the price.

J. B. LIPPINCOTT COMPANY,
715 and 717 Market Street, Philadelphia.

American Novels, No. 1.

THE DESERTER AND FROM THE RANKS.

By CAPTAIN CHARLES KING,
Author of "The Colonel's Daughter," "Marion's Faith," etc.

COMPLETE IN ONE VOLUME.

Square 12mo. Extra cloth, $1.00. Paper, 50 cents.

"Captain King is one of the best of modern writers of military fiction, worthy to rank on this side the water with John Strange Winter on the other. His pictures of army life impress one by their manifest sincerity, their dramatic interest, and their wholesome and manly motives. These two stories have a tone and an atmosphere wholly different from the commonplace novel of the day, and for that reason alone they are highly enjoyable."—*Boston Literary World.*

"The gallant captain has all a soldier's generous enthusiasm for lovely woman and the delights of a cosy, love-lit home, and his heroines are all sweet, wholesome women that do honor to his heart and pen. These two stories are bright and interesting, and we heartily recommend them to public favor."—*Germantown Telegraph.*

"Captain King surpasses any other writer of army life that we have yet had, and his sketches of society life and character at the military stations in the far West are as brilliant as they are entertaining. The plots of both these stories are ingeniously conceived and skilfully carried out, and they are replete with stirring and exciting incidents."—*Boston Home Journal.*

"The author has had the good sense to select a department of fiction which he is excellently fitted to describe. There is just enough of wholesome plot in 'The Deserter' and 'From the Ranks' to keep the reader's interest unabated to the end. The tone of the work is fresh and charming. Captain King has a quick and sentient touch, and his writing is that of one whose belief in mankind is untouched by bitterness. One reads his tales with the satisfying sense of a cheerful solution of all difficulties on the final page. It is a relief, indeed, to turn from the dismal introspection of much of our modern fiction to the fresh naturalness of such stories as these."—*New York Critic.*

"The author of 'The Colonel's Daughter' has studied the intrigues, jealousies, and romances of army life on the spot, and draws life-like portraits of favorite officers and men, of overbearing captains' wives and sisters, and describes the monotonous camp-life and its sudden dangers truthfully."—*New York Publishers' Weekly.*

"He tells his stories with so much spirit that one's interest is maintained to the end. The character-studies are good and the plot cleverly developed."—*New York Book-Buyer.*

"The characters are all truly soldierly men, of no low rank in the American army. There is plenty of intrigue in the plot to show that there is more than one kind of an explosive in a camp. The society, life, and amusements of this certain class of people are very clearly brought to light, and if it were not for the positive fact that they exist only in fiction, one could easily imagine that they were real persons, so natural and real do their actions seem. The reader can gain several new ideas in regard to the pleasures of those in the army as well as an idea of some of the dangers that constantly threaten the officers, from Captain King's full description of them."—*Boston Herald.*

⁂ For sale by all Booksellers, or will be sent, post-paid, on receipt of the price.

J. B. LIPPINCOTT COMPANY, Publishers,
715 and 717 Market Street, Philadelphia.

American Novels, No. 2.

BRUETON'S BAYOU,

By JOHN HABBERTON, author of "Helen's Babies,"

AND

MISS DEFARGE,

By FRANCES HODGSON BURNETT, author of "That Lass o' Lowries."

COMPLETE IN ONE VOLUME.

Square 12mo. Extra cloth, $1.00. Paper, 50 cents.

"A good book to put in the satchel for a railway trip or ocean voyage."—*Chicago Current.*

"In every way worthy of the best of our American story-writers."—*Washington Public Opinion.*

"It is safe to say that no two more charming stories were ever bound in one cover than these."—*New Orleans Picayune.*

"Two thoroughly good and entertaining American novels. The literary character of the authors will attract every cultivated reader."—*Boston Globe.*

"We are glad to have 'Brueton's Bayou' in our hands again,—to recall its charming picture of Southern life, with the genuine naturalness of that simple household and the subtle differences in the social virtues and exactions of two extremes of civilization. Everything about the story is charming, from the sweet dignity of the impulsive Velce and the instinctive cleverness of her old darkey protector, to the gentle irony which occasionally displays itself in the description of the men of the plantation. In 'Miss Defarge' Mrs. Burnett has given us a good deal of action and that vigorous handling which has become characteristic of her late style."—*New York Critic.*

"Two more delightful stories than these it were hard to find. The reputation of Mr. Habberton and Mrs. Burnett are guarantee that there isn't a dull line in either of these works. They will be welcomed heartily, and read again and again."—*Nashville American.*

"Two pleasing stories. Mrs. Burnett's stories are always bright and interesting, and 'Brueton's Bayou' is readable from cover to cover."—*Baltimore American.*

"'Brueton's Bayou' is an excellent tale, the motive of which is apparently to instil into the haughty insularity of the New York mind a realizing sense of the intellectual possibilities of the Southwest. The smug and self-satisfied young New York business-man, who is detained by the lameness of his horse at Brueton's Bayou, and there presently meets his fate in the form of a brilliant and beautiful girl of the region, has the nonsense taken out of him very thoroughly by his Southern experiences. 'Miss Defarge' is a strong study of a very resolute and self-centred young woman, who accomplishes many things by sheer force of will. But the most interesting and charming figure in it is that of Elizabeth Dysart, the blonde beauty, a kind of modernized Dudu,— 'large and languishing and lazy,'—but of a sweetness of temper and general lovableness not to be surpassed."—*New York Tribune.*

*** For sale by all Booksellers, or will be sent, post-paid, on receipt of the price.

J. B. LIPPINCOTT COMPANY, Publishers,

715 and 717 Market Street, Philadelphia.

American Novels, No. 3.

SINFIRE,

By JULIAN HAWTHORNE, author of "Archibald Malmaison," etc.

AND

DOUGLAS DUANE,

By EDGAR FAWCETT, author of "A Gentleman of Leisure," etc.

COMPLETE IN ONE VOLUME.

Square 12mo. Extra cloth, $1.00. Paper, 50 cents.

"The style is unique, the incident thrilling, and a weird and fantastic thread runs through both the stories."—*Norristown Herald.*

"They are tales of the most marvellous nature, but with enough of the possible, every-day life interwoven so skilfully that the interest is kept up throughout."—*Portland Transcript.*

"Both are curious, picturesque stories, well worked out, and among the author's most popular efforts."—*New York Graphic.*

"Two novels that have been well received and that are very warmly praised."—*Boston Transcript.*

"These are novels by two of the most popular writers of the day. Each is thoroughly imbued with the deep interest peculiar to its author."—*Boston Home Journal.*

"Both of the stories are well worth perusal."—*Kansas City Times.*

For sale by all Booksellers, or will be sent, post-paid, on receipt of the price.

J. B. LIPPINCOTT COMPANY, PUBLISHERS,

715 and 717 Market Street,

Philadelphia, Pa.

Picked Up in the Streets.

FROM THE GERMAN OF H. SCHOBERT.

Translated by Mrs. A. L. WISTER.

12mo.   Extra Cloth. $1.25.

"An entertaining, romantic story, with a healthy moral. The pathos is genuine, and those who figure in it are unexaggerated types of human nature. It may be read with profit and pleasure by old and young."—*Boston Gazette.*

"It is a romance of more than usual interest. Like so many novels of the epoch, it is Russian in motive, but the scenes are laid in France and Germany. The characters in the story are so high-spirited and intensely aristocratic in their way that loves and hates, plots and counterplots, and, above all, the duel, will be deliciously pleasing to simple republicans. But the story has even a greater merit than its interest—it is not too long."—*Philadelphia Times.*

"You read on; things become interesting; the 'plot thickens, new elements are drawn into it; new contingencies—new impossibilities—emerge, to be resolved after much bitterness into sweet harmonies and things altogether possible. Two or three strong characters stand aloof and aloft, and show that Herr Schobert has a sharp power of analysis and characterization, and that his Germans and Russians are not walking and talking puppets. The court life at a petty German principality is admirably depicted; not less so the courtiers and princelings, and the strong, luminous figure of the heroine. Mrs. Wister translates with delightful ease, and brings all these things before us as if she were composing originally, and not translating."—*N. Y. Critic.*

"As a romancer H. Schobert expresses himself with delicacy. His ideas of life are not overwrought, although at times they assume a highly sensational character. The interest of his story centres in his picturesque and realistic views of society life at the German court, where the prominent scenes are mostly laid. He has the power to shift from one scene to another without disturbing the harmony of the whole, and, with Mrs. Wister as a translator, his work cannot fail to find favor."—*Boston Herald.*

"Like all of Mrs. Wister's translations, it is spirited and entertaining."—*Toledo Blade.*

⁎ For sale by all Booksellers, or will be sent, post-paid, on receipt of the price by the publishers.

THE
OWL'S NEST.
BY E. MARLITT.
TRANSLATED BY MRS. A. L. WISTER.

12mo.   Extra cloth, $1.25.

"The best story which Mrs. Wister has translated for some years. It has all the sentimental qualities dear to the German heart and much of the *esprit* demanded by American taste. The moral is excellent, inculcating the precept that girls must *seem* as well as *be* irreproachable in behavior."—*Philadelphia Ledger.*

"The book is as sweet and wholesome as its predecessors. . . . The descriptions of scenery are alone enough to reward one for reading the book. They are so vivid that one can almost smell the pines and feel the blowing wind."—*Boston Globe.*

"This story has the minute delicacy and graphic simplicity of all of Marlitt's stories, and it is gracefully translated."—*New York Independent.*

"These translations are gaining a place among the standard literature of the day. Pure in thought, not extravagant in tone, they portray human nature as we each day see it around us. The pictures of German life, whether among peasantry or those of the high degree, are both pleasing and instructive, and the moral such as will be an influence for good."—*Norristown Herald.*

"It has the same elements of strength and interest, the same effective blending of the subjects of romance with the methods of realism, that we find in all the novels of this author coming through the hands of this translator."—*American Bookseller.*

For sale by all Booksellers, or will be sent, post-paid, on receipt of price.

J. B. LIPPINCOTT COMPANY, PUBLISHERS,
715 and 717 Market Street,
Philadelphia, Pa.

CHOICE GERMAN FICTION.

MRS. WISTER'S TRANSLATIONS.

It is generally acknowledged that Mrs. Wister's literary judgment is of the highest order, and that she possesses an unfailing tact for selecting only such German novels as are well adapted to please the American taste. This, together with the rare excellence of her translations, and her peculiar power of infusing her spirit into them, imparting to every story she undertakes a distinctive individuality and charm, renders her works among the most popular of the day.

THE OWL'S NEST	$1 25
PICKED UP IN THE STREETS	1 25
THE ALPINE FAY	1 25
SAINT MICHAEL	1 25
THE LADY WITH THE RUBIES	1 25
A PENNILESS GIRL	1 25
BANNED AND BLESSED	1 50
FROM HAND TO HAND	1 50
THE EICHHOFS	1 50
CASTLE HOHENWALD	1 50
TOO RICH	1 50
THE GREEN GATE	1 50
WHY DID HE NOT DIE?	1 50
THE BAILIFF'S MAID	1 25
AT THE COUNCILLOR'S	1 50
THE OLD MAM'SELLE'S SECRET	1 50
COUNTESS GISELA	1 50
VIOLETTA	1 25
VAIN FOREBODINGS	1 25
QUICKSANDS	1 50
A NOBLE NAME	1 50
SEVERA	1 50
A NEW RACE	1 25
MARGARETHE	1 50
A FAMILY FEUD	1 25
ONLY A GIRL	1 50
HULDA	1 50
IN THE SCHILLINGSCOURT	1 50
THE SECOND WIFE	1 50
GOLD ELSIE	1 50
THE LITTLE MOORLAND PRINCESS	1 50

Complete sets of the above in 20 volumes, bound in uniform and attractive style, can be had for $29.00

*** For sale by all Booksellers, or will be sent, post-paid, on receipt of the price, by

J. B. LIPPINCOTT COMPANY, Publishers,
Nos. 715 and 717 Market St., Philadelphia.

MRS. H. LOVETT CAMERON'S NOVELS.

16mo. Half cloth, 50 cents. Paper cover, 25 cents.

A LIFE'S MISTAKE.

Mrs. Cameron is a vivacious, entertaining, and pure writer. The plot and movement of her stories are interesting, and they are all deservedly popular.

WORTH WINNING.

"A story that is well calculated to hold the reader's interest from beginning to end. The style is good."—*Savannah News.*

"A very interesting story of English life, the characters being well sketched and the plot skilfully developed."—*Washington (D.C.) Public Opinion.*

VERA NEVILL;
Or, Poor Wisdom's Chance.

"There is unusual force in this novel. The character of the heroine is drawn with great power, while the incidents fit into each other with rare skill, leading up to the dénouement with an artistic fitness not often seen."—*Peterson's Magazine.*

"Is intensely dramatic. The style throughout is bright and readable."—*San Francisco Chronicle.*

PURE GOLD.

"It is well written, and the book throughout is thoroughly interesting."—*Boston Globe.*

"It is an interesting story."—*Baltimore American.*

"A good old English story of the present day, and can be read with profit."—*St. Louis Republican.*

IN A GRASS COUNTRY.
A Story of Love and Sport.

"Is so fresh and fascinating that one cannot easily be tempted to lay the book aside without having read it from cover to cover."—*Boston Advertiser.*

"Is an uncommonly good story of love and sport. It is, first of all, entertaining. There is not a dull line in the whole story, nor a paragraph to be skipped. The book is full of merriment."—*New York Critic.*

⁎ For sale by all Booksellers, or will be sent by mail, postage prepaid, on receipt of the price by the publishers.

THE JEWEL IN THE LOTOS

A NOVEL.

By MARY AGNES TINCKER,

Author of "Aurora," "Signor Monaldini's Niece," etc.

With Five Handsome Illustrations by Thomas and Helen C. Hovenden.

12mo. Extra cloth. $1.25.

"There is not a dull page in it. Every one in this novel, from Glenlyon to the servants in the kitchen, has his separate and rounded individuality. It is full of beautiful pictures, and has certain passages we should be glad to quote, but we must be content to leave these to the reader to discover."—*The Literary World*.

"A very pleasant novel to read, and one that once begun will be finished by the reader. It is peculiarly fresh and breezy and out of doors."—*St. Louis Republican*.

"There are charming descriptions of Italian scenery in this novel, excellent drawings of titled and peasant folk, some good character sketches of English people, and satire that is delicate and true. But the most interesting part is the Catholicism."—*New York Times*.

"Never was a book written that contained more charming descriptive passages. Here and there through the book they appear like pictures illuminating the story and happily transporting the writer to the Italian country."—*New Orleans Picayune*.

"The story is an intensely interesting one, the plot is strong, the characters natural, and the style clear, graceful, and attractive. It is a work which will be read with profit as well as pleasure in every home."—*Baltimore Evening News*.

"It is a strong novel, full of human nature and passion, with a spice of the romantic in the way of the disputed birth of the heroine and a band of mounted bandits."—*San Francisco Chronicle*.

"A novel of more than usual interest."—*Springfield Republican*.

"An Italian tale of the highest order of literary merit. The pictures of life in the land of bright skies and dark deeds are powerfully drawn, as with a masculine hand, while the emotions are played upon with a touch delicately feminine. The language is as fluent as the discernment is keen, and the reader is carried along by an easy progress through the details of a rather sad plot as smoothly as the glide of a gondola on a Venetian canal, constantly enjoying sensations as grateful as the balmy air that soothes the feelings in the land of history and of romance. It is a valuable addition to the literature of the day."—*Pittsburgh Commercial-Gazette*.

www.ingramcontent.com/pod-product-compliance
Lightning Source LLC
Chambersburg PA
CBHW032106230426
43672CB00009B/1653